STAR WARS

CLONE WARS
ADVENTURES
VOLUME 9

APPETITE FOR ADVENTURE
script and art **The Fillbach Brothers**
colors **Ronda Pattison**

SALVAGED
script and art **The Fillbach Brothers**
colors **Pamela Rambo**

LIFE BELOW
script and art **The Fillbach Brothers**
colors **Dan Jackson**
with Madigan Jackson

NO WAY OUT
script and art **The Fillbach Brothers**
colors **Tony Avina**

lettering
Michael Heisler

cover
The Fillbach Brothers and Dan Jackson

Dark Horse Books®

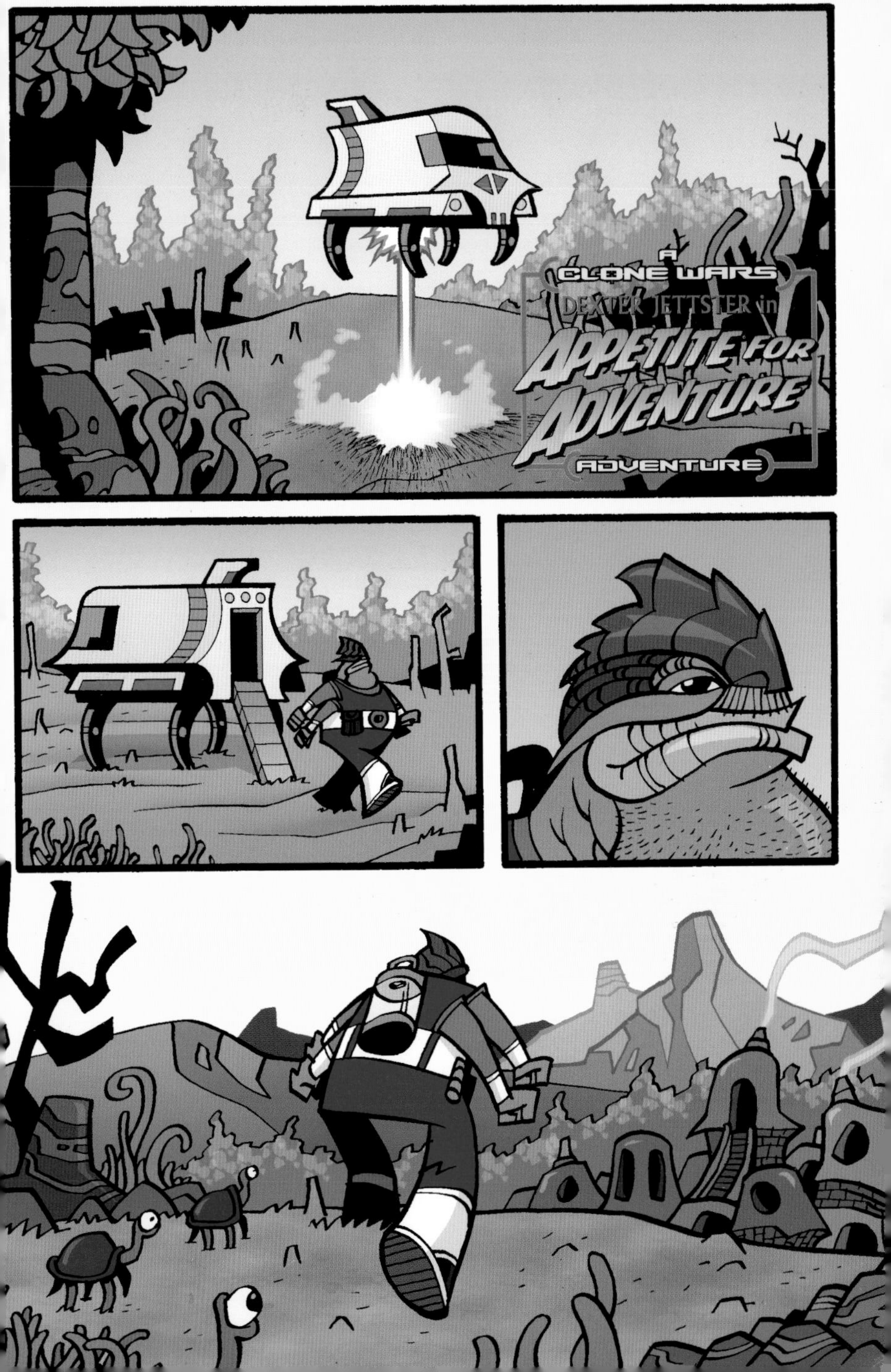
A
CLONE WARS
DEXTER JETTSTER in
APPETITE FOR ADVENTURE
ADVENTURE

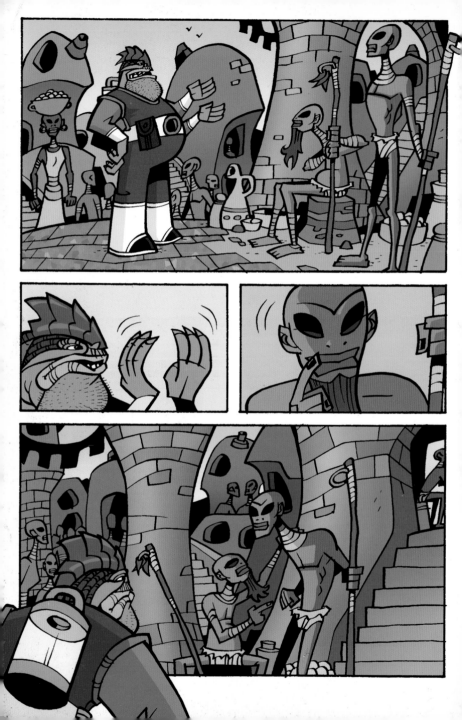

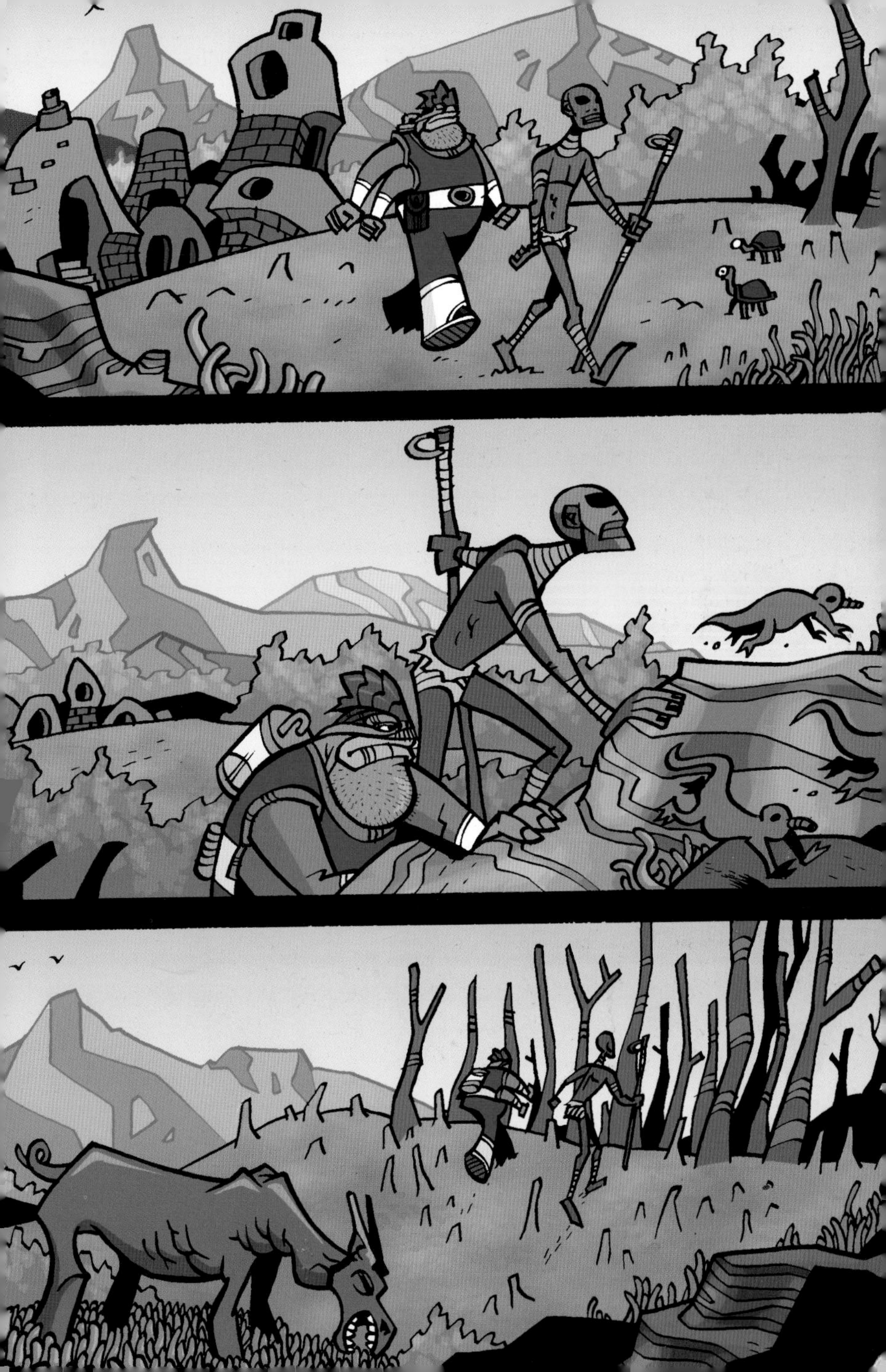

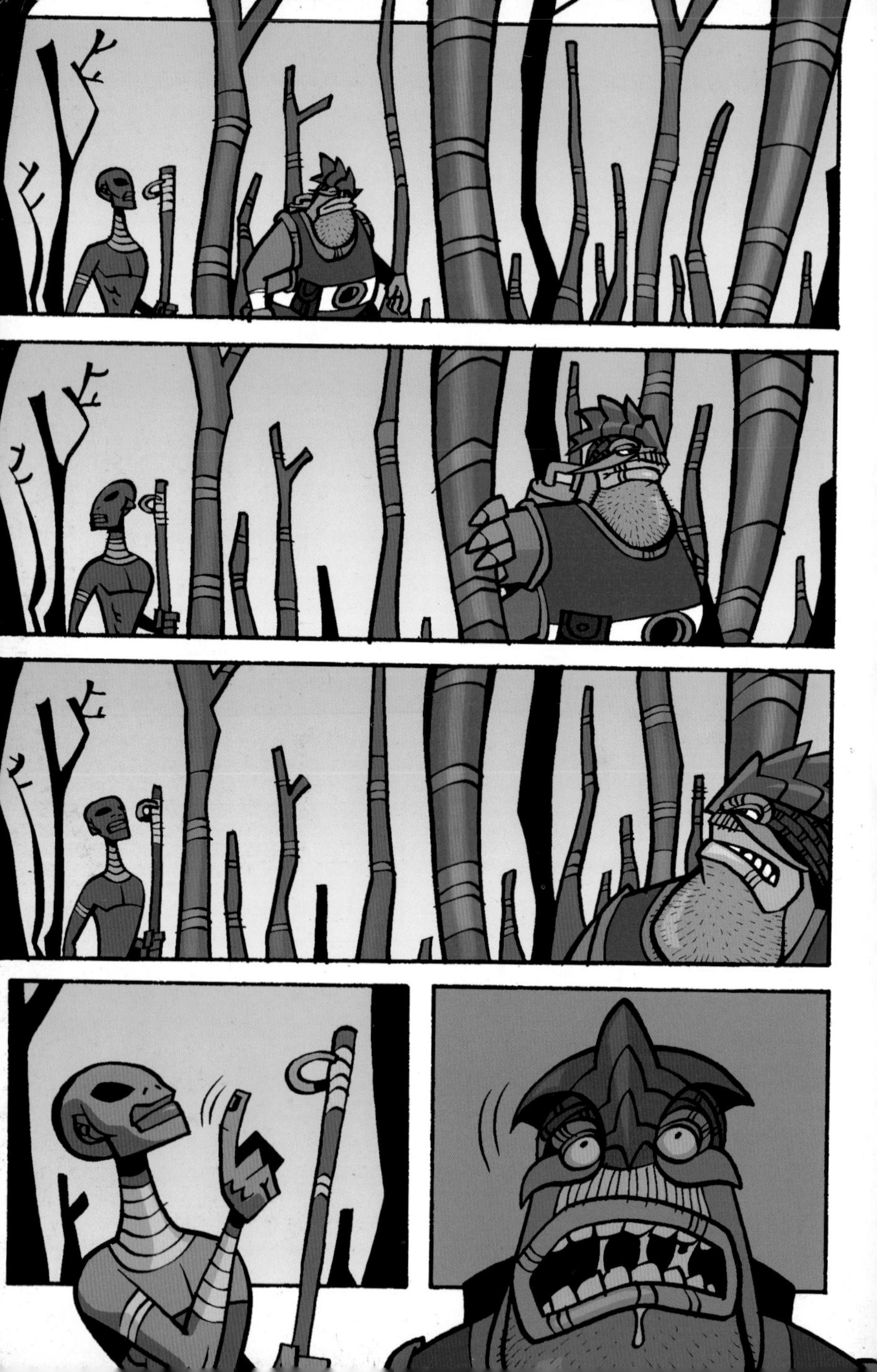

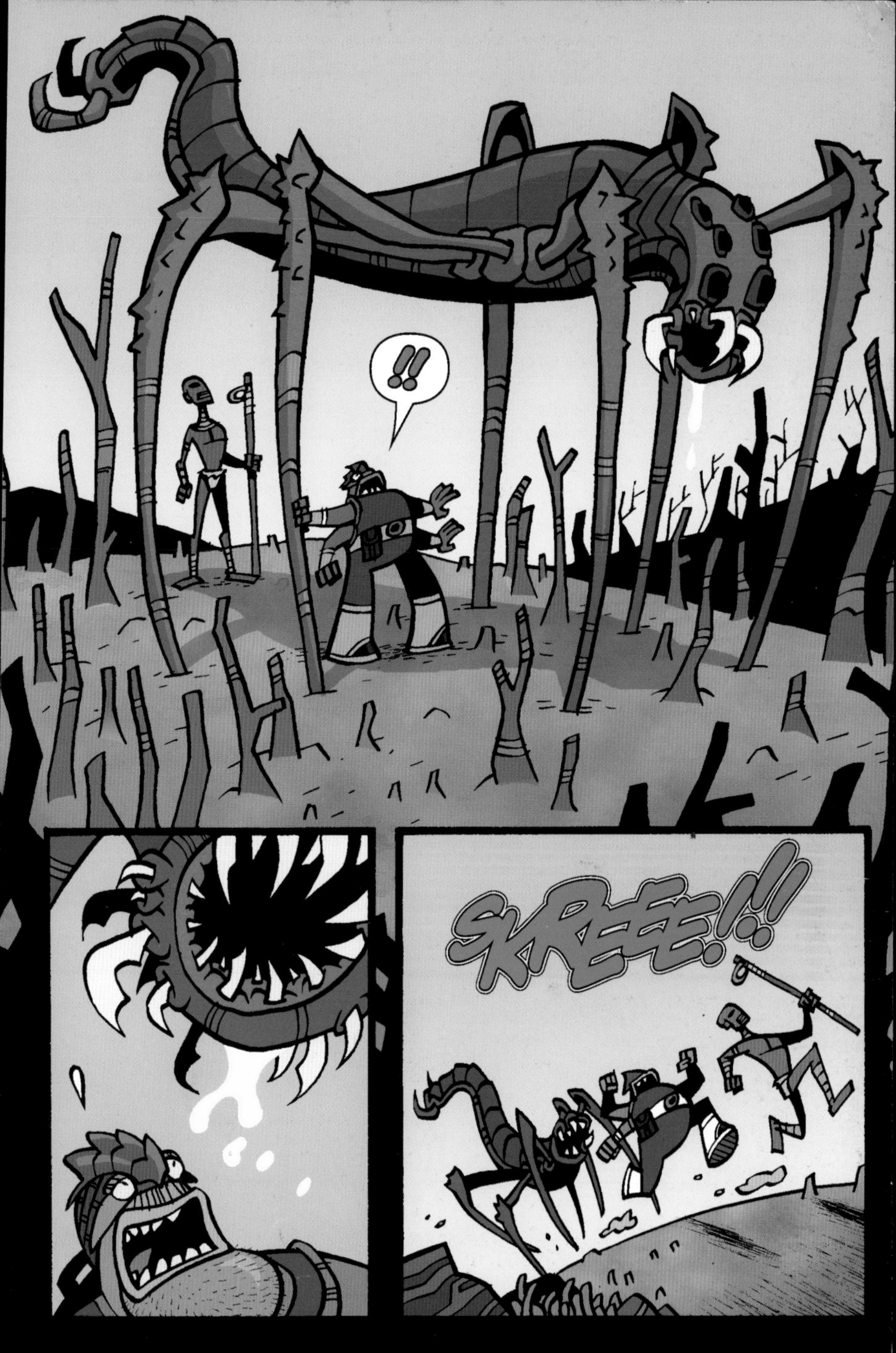
!!
SKREEE!!!

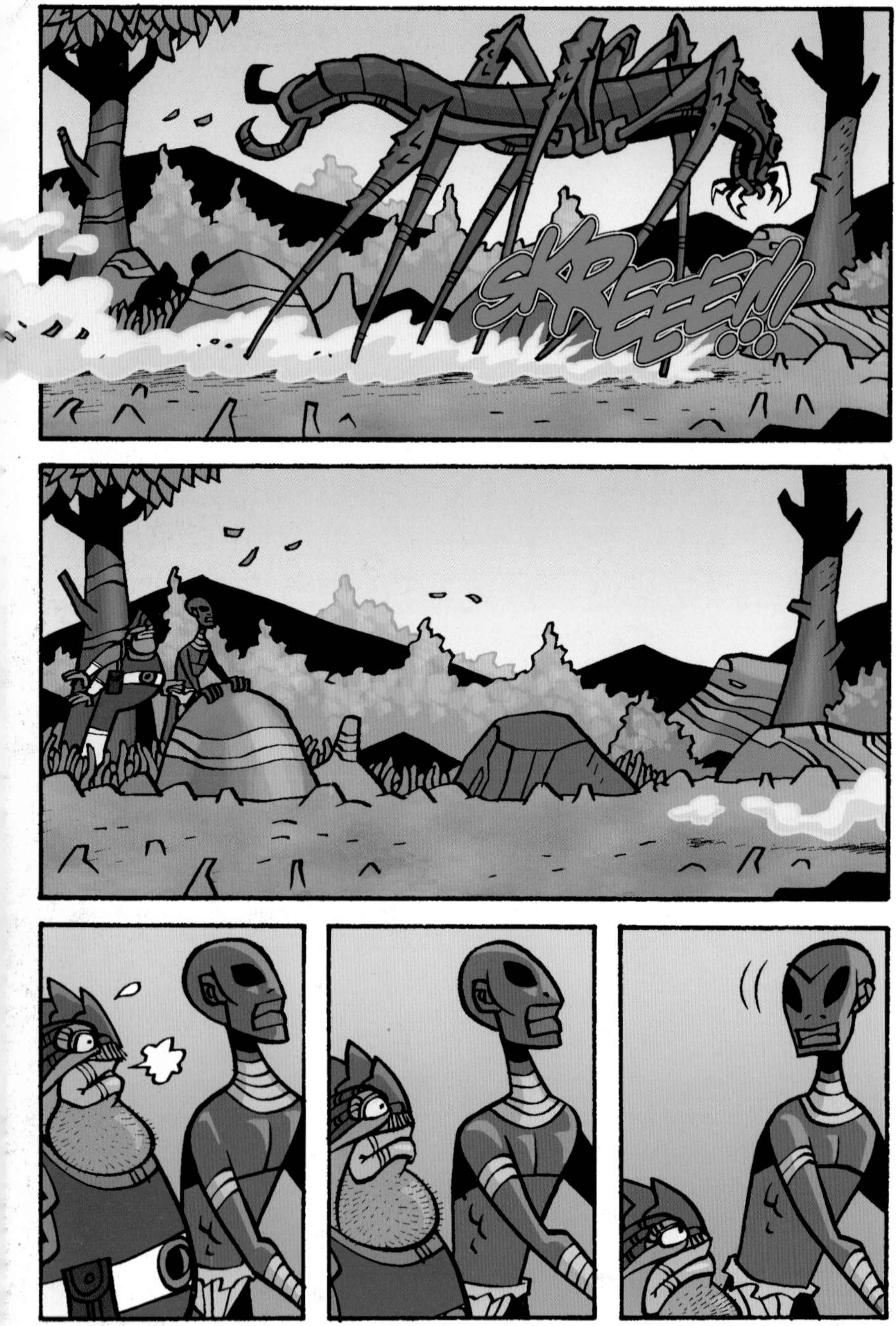
SKREEEE!!!

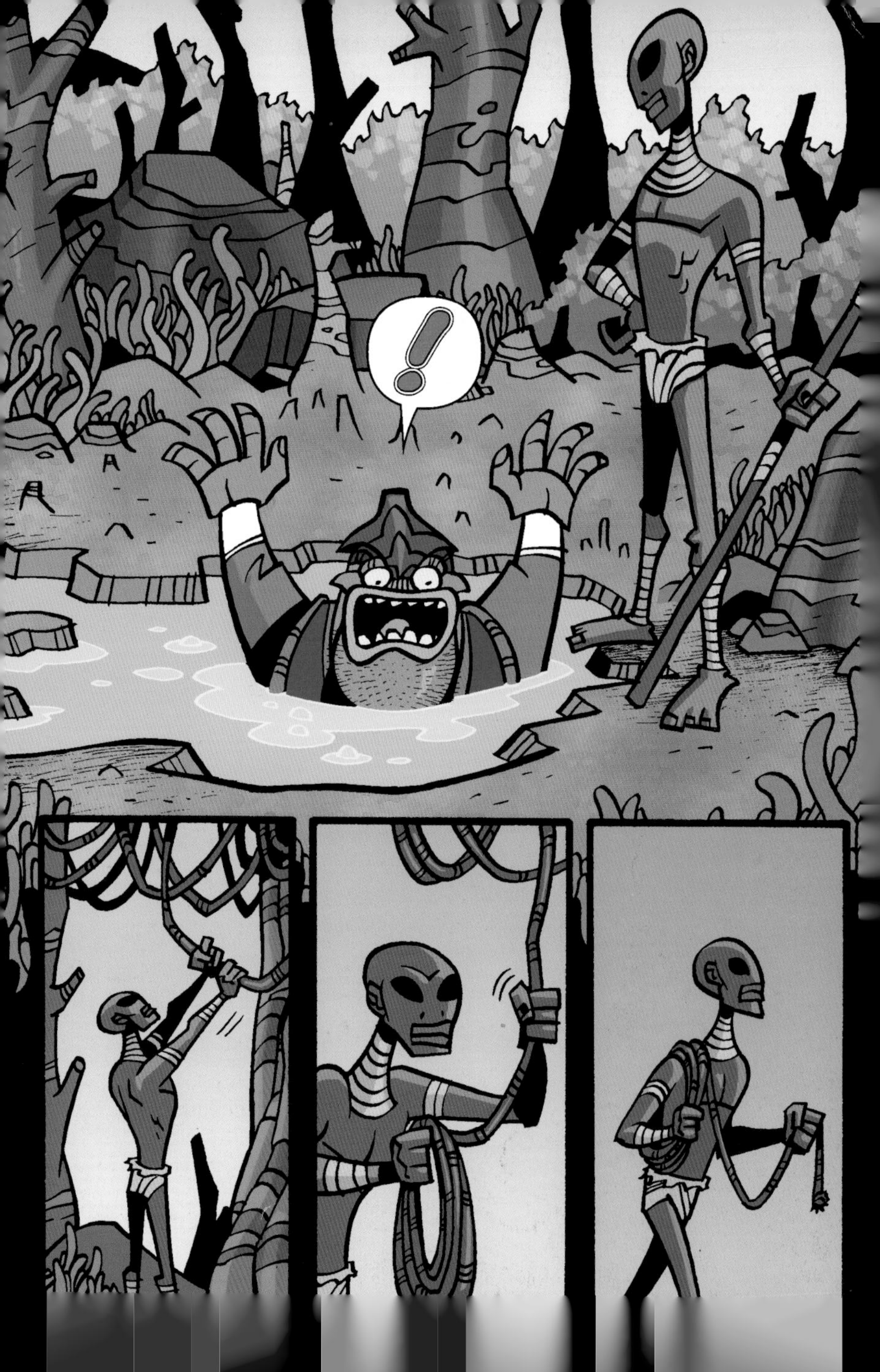
!

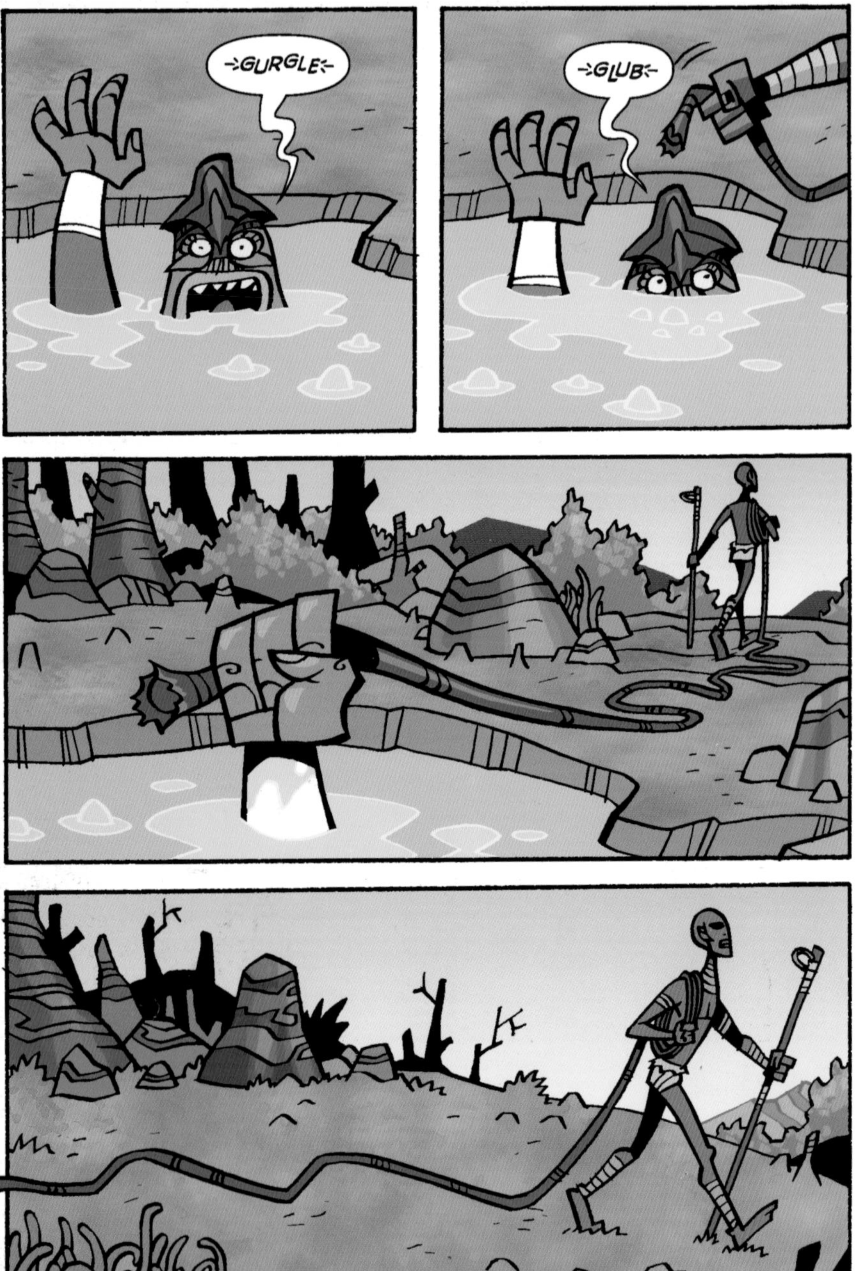
GURGLE
GLUB

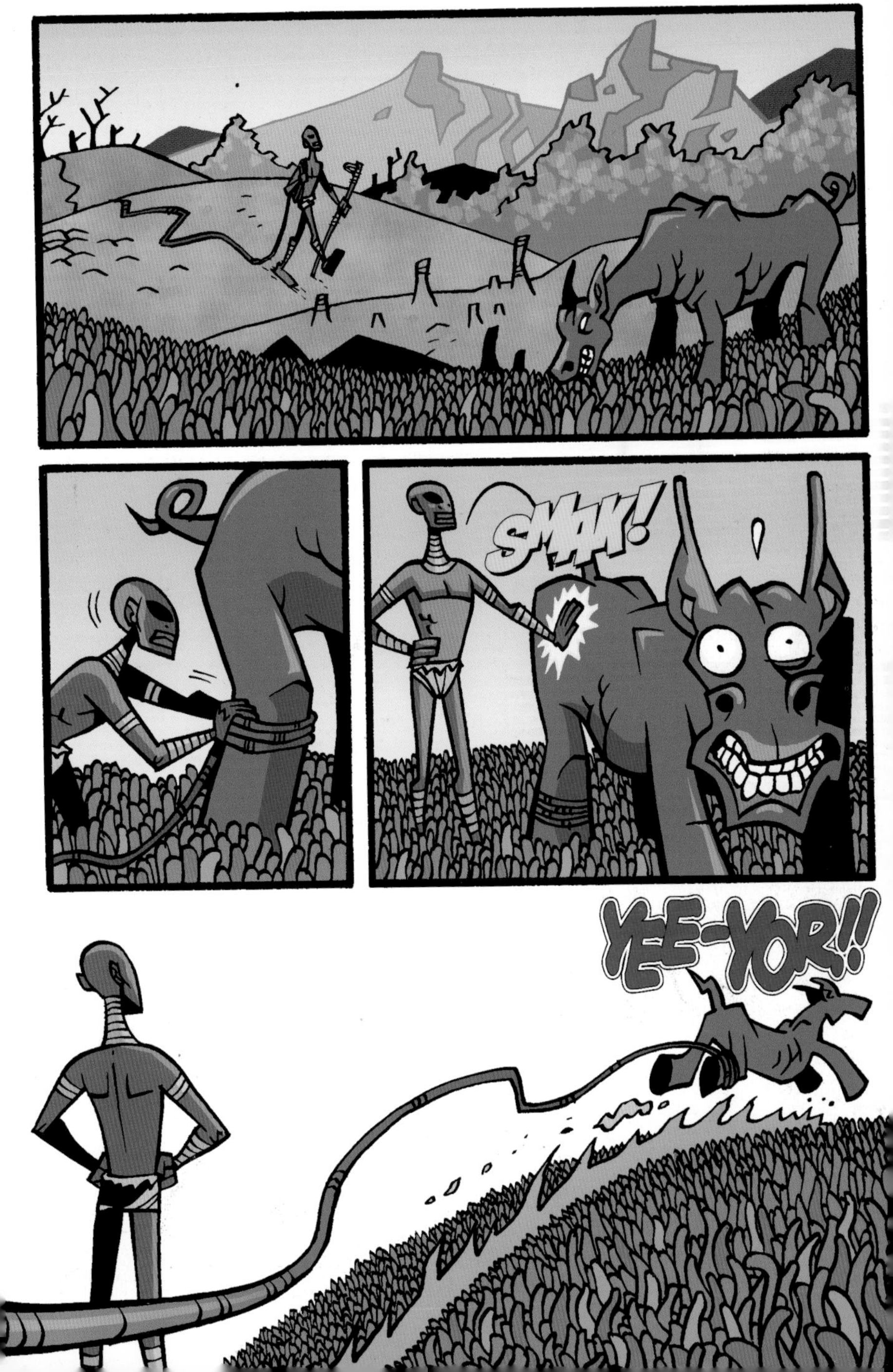
SMAK!
YEE-YOR!!

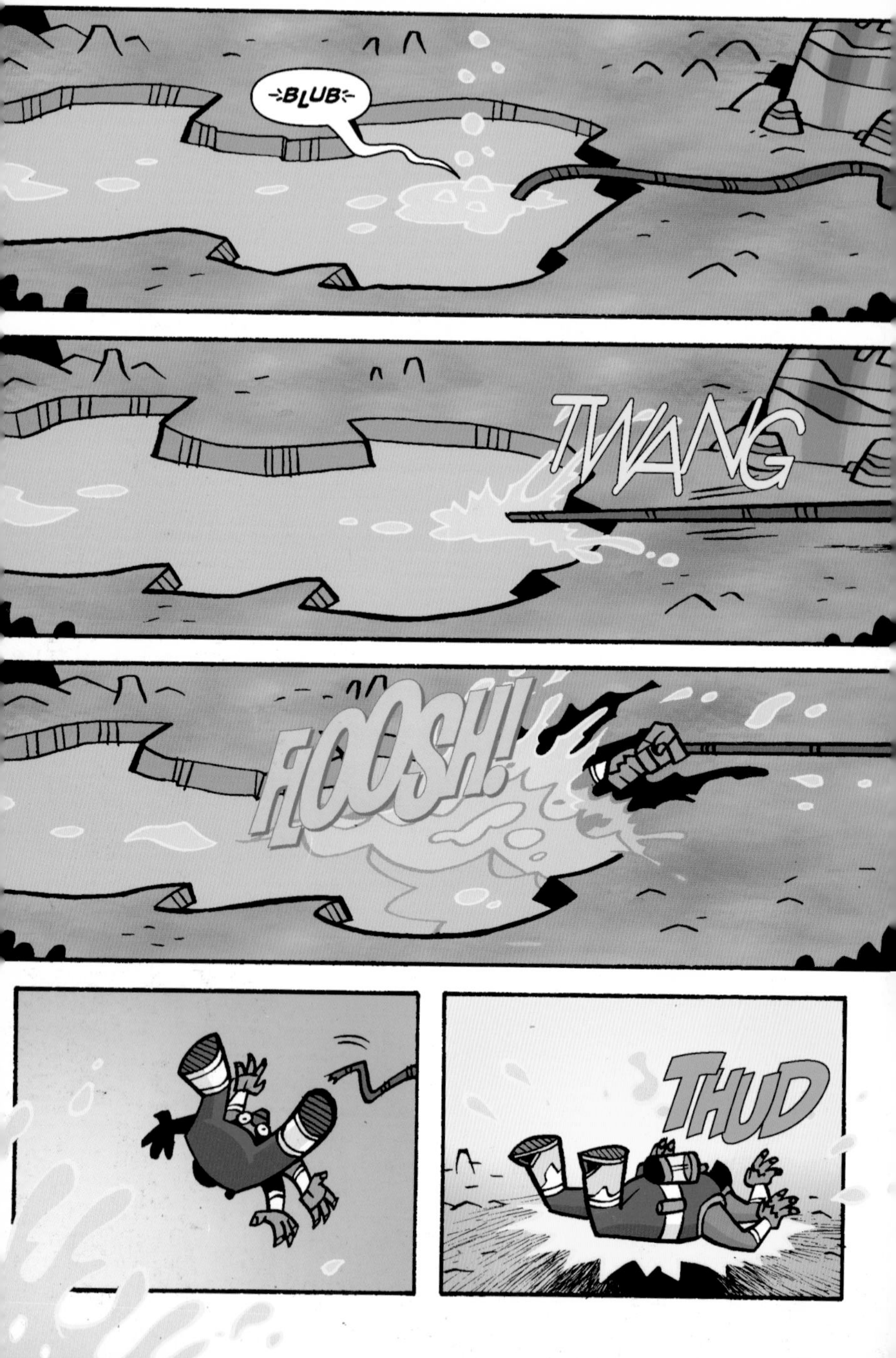
BLUB
TWANG
FLOOSH!
THUD

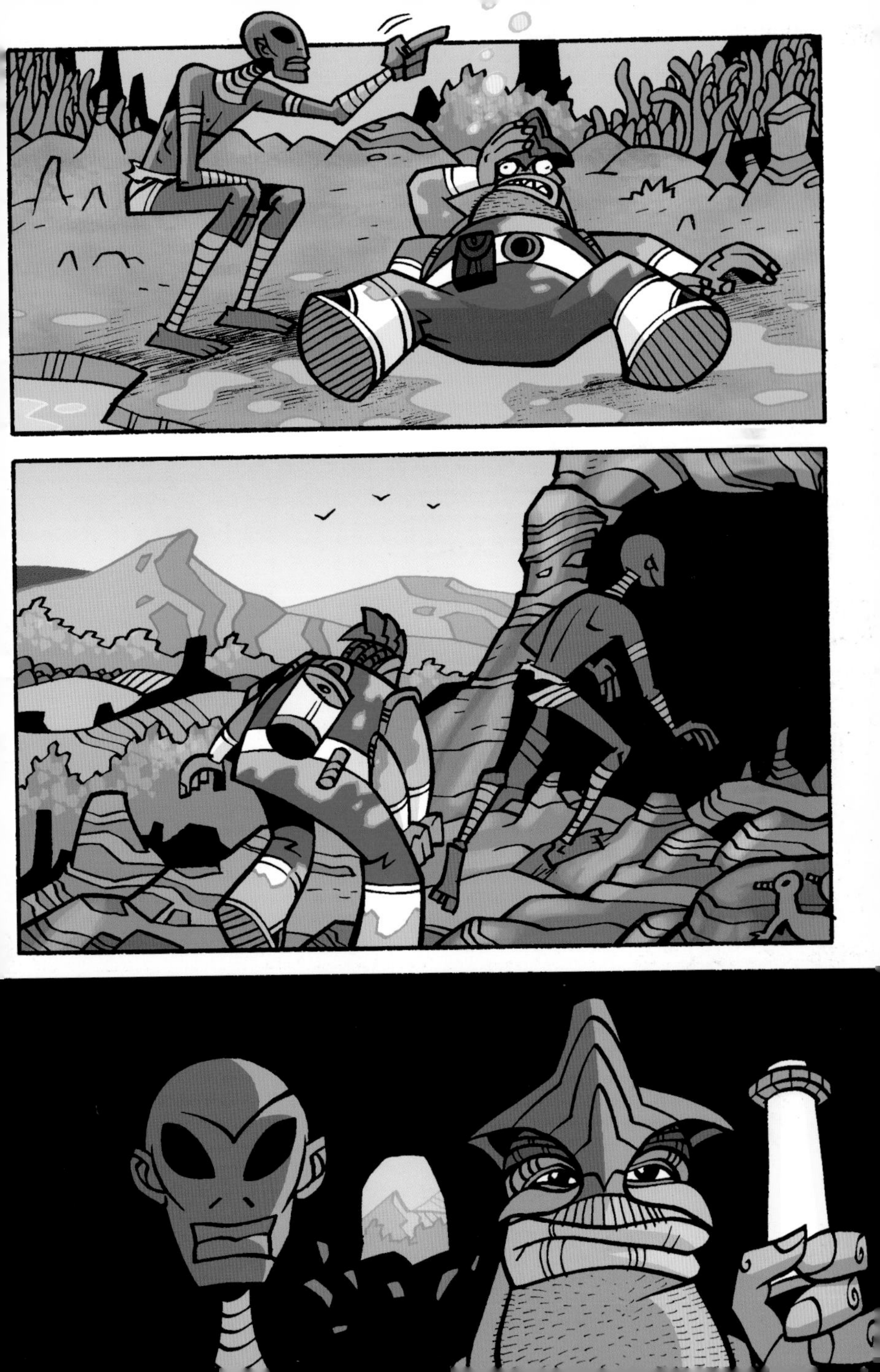

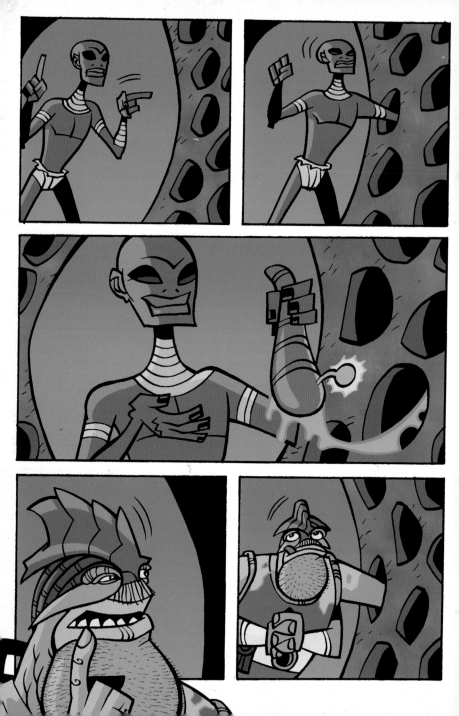

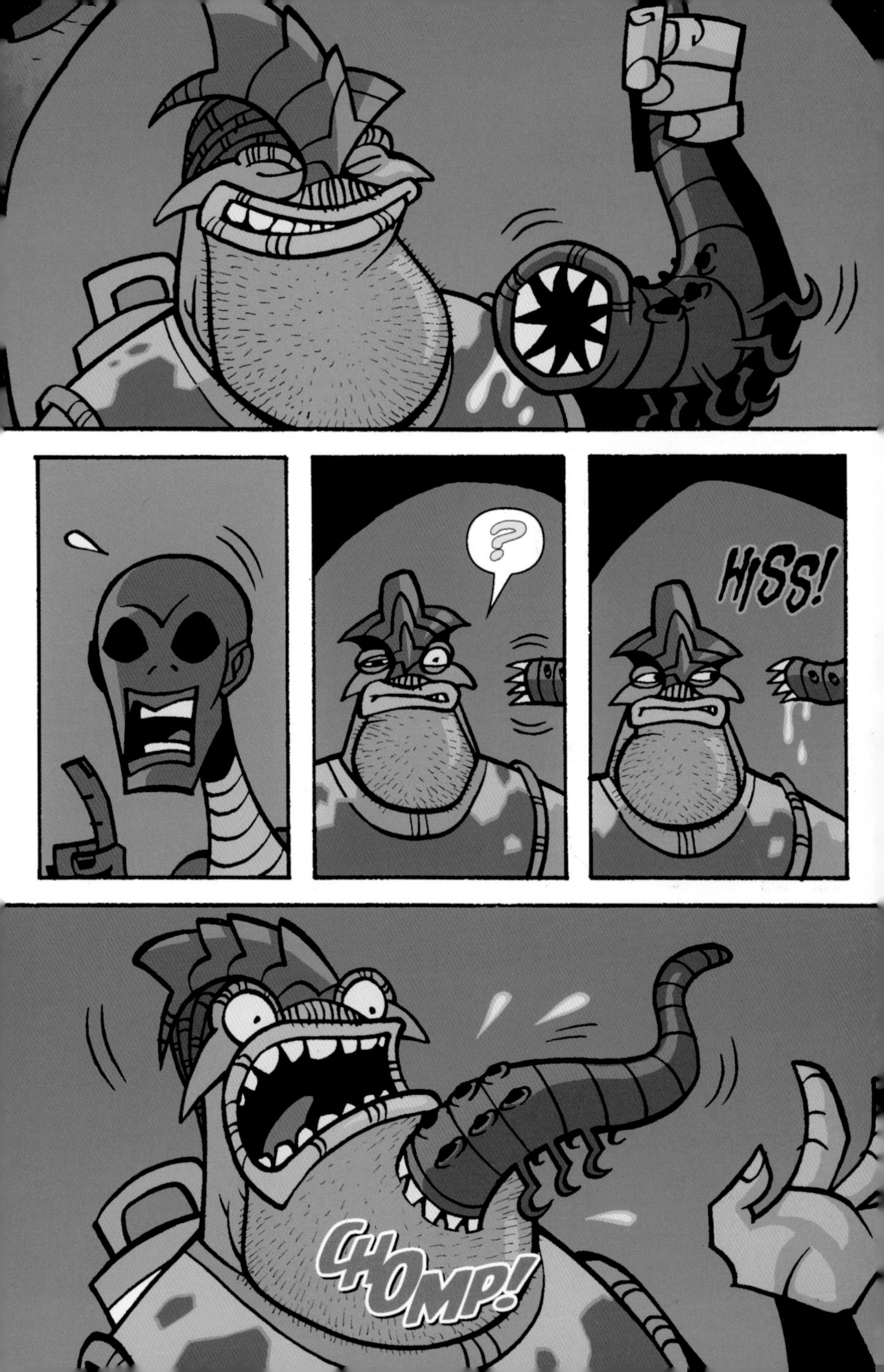
?
HISS!
CHOMP!

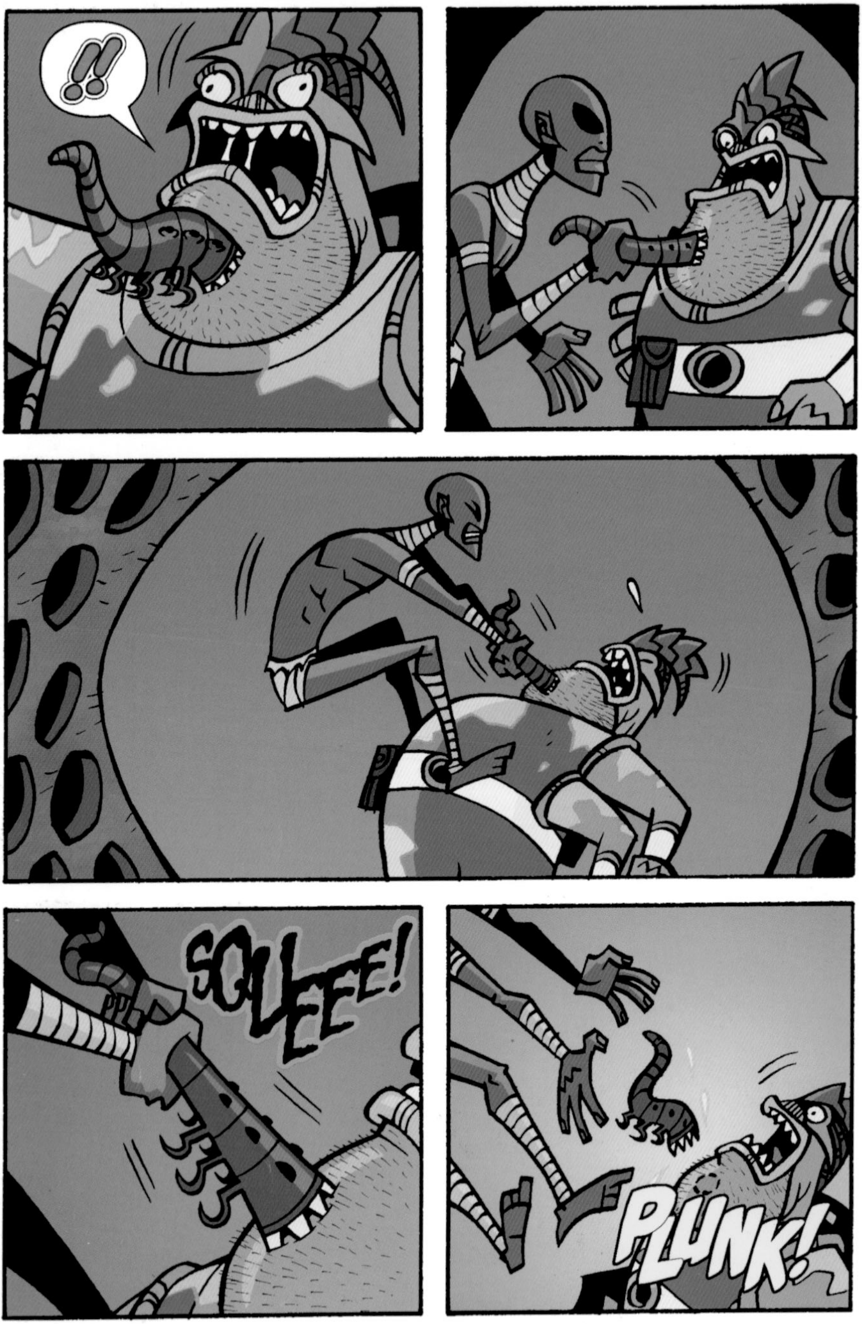
!!
SQLEEE!
PLUNK!

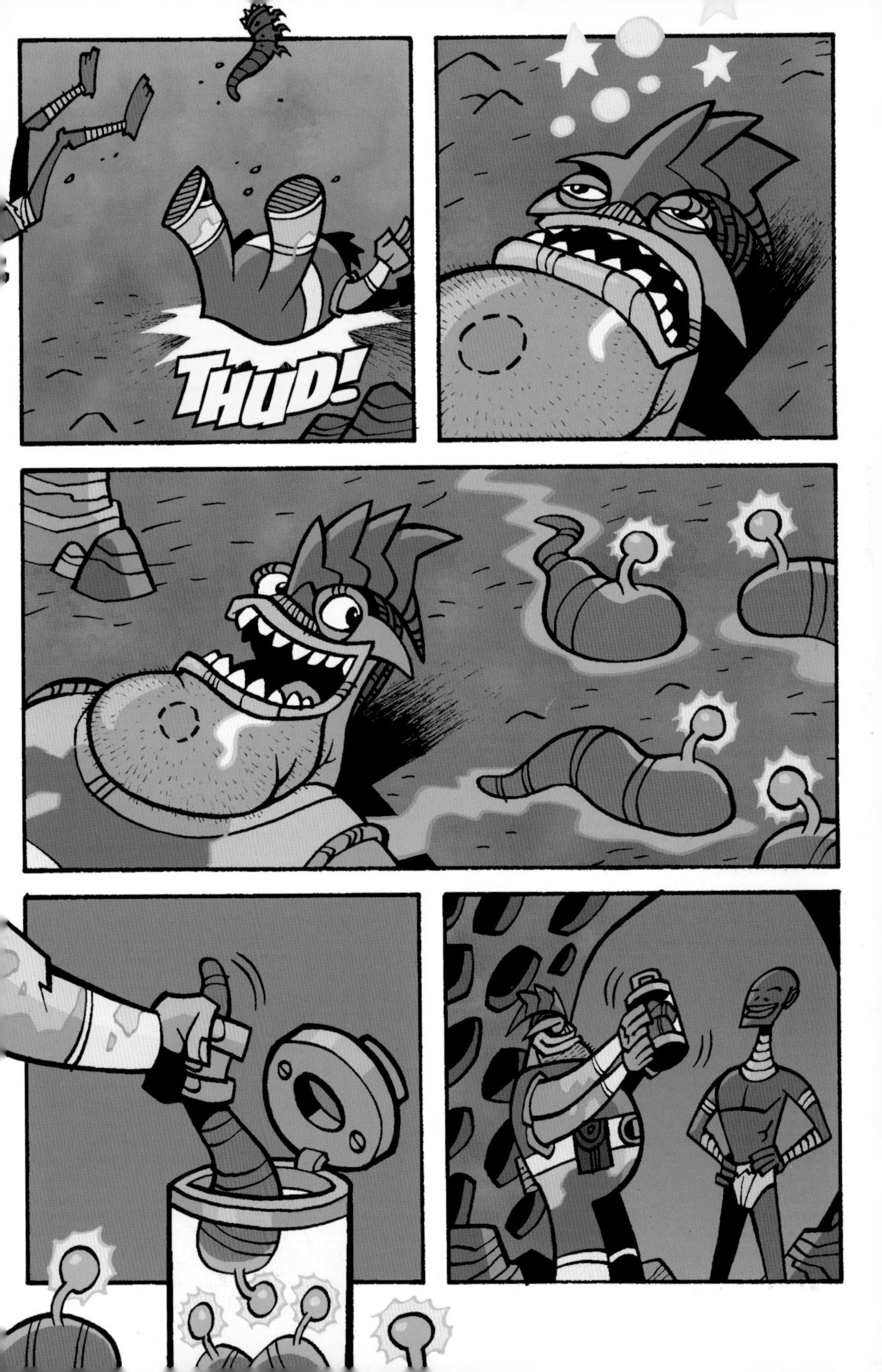
THUD!

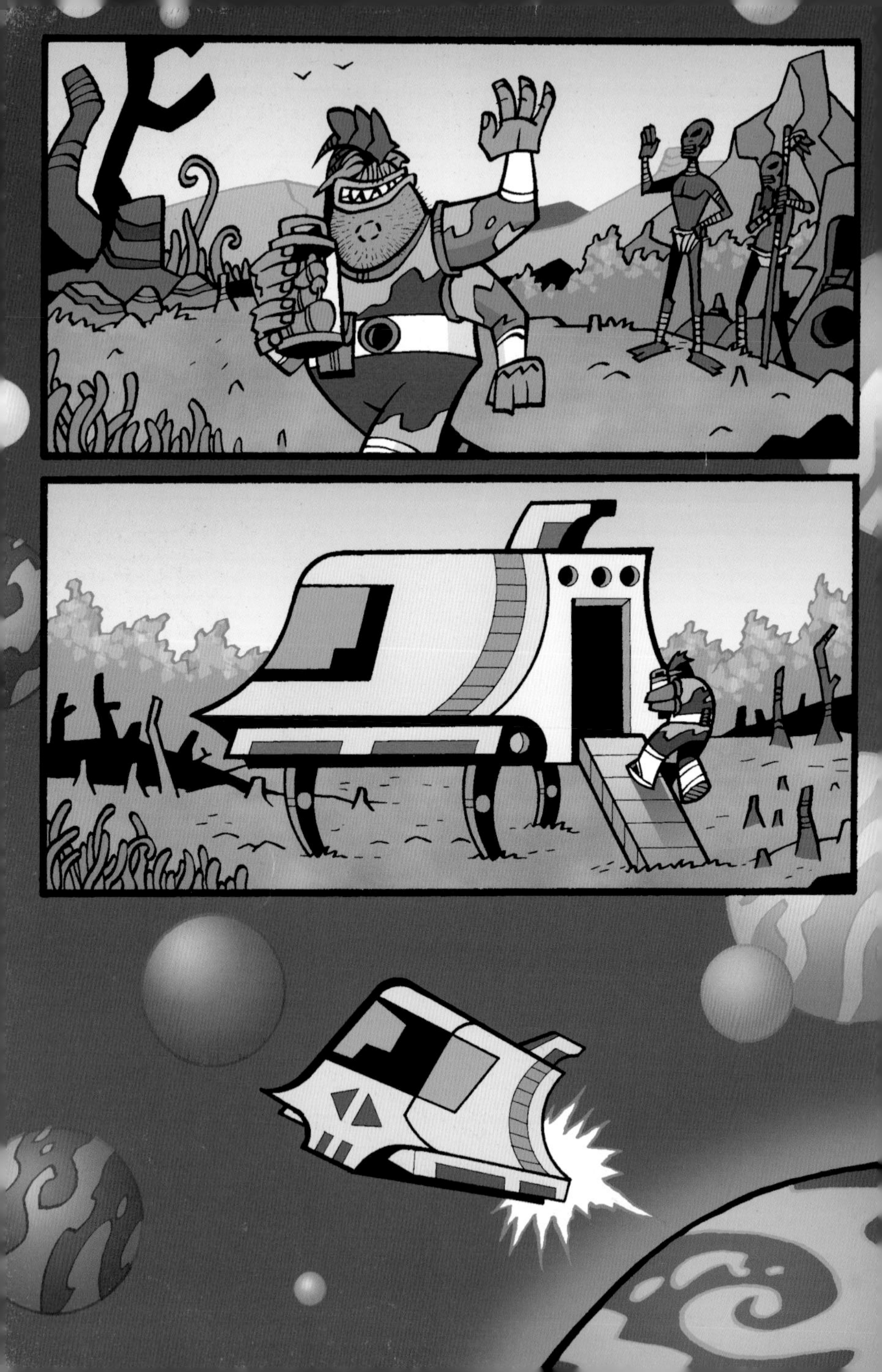

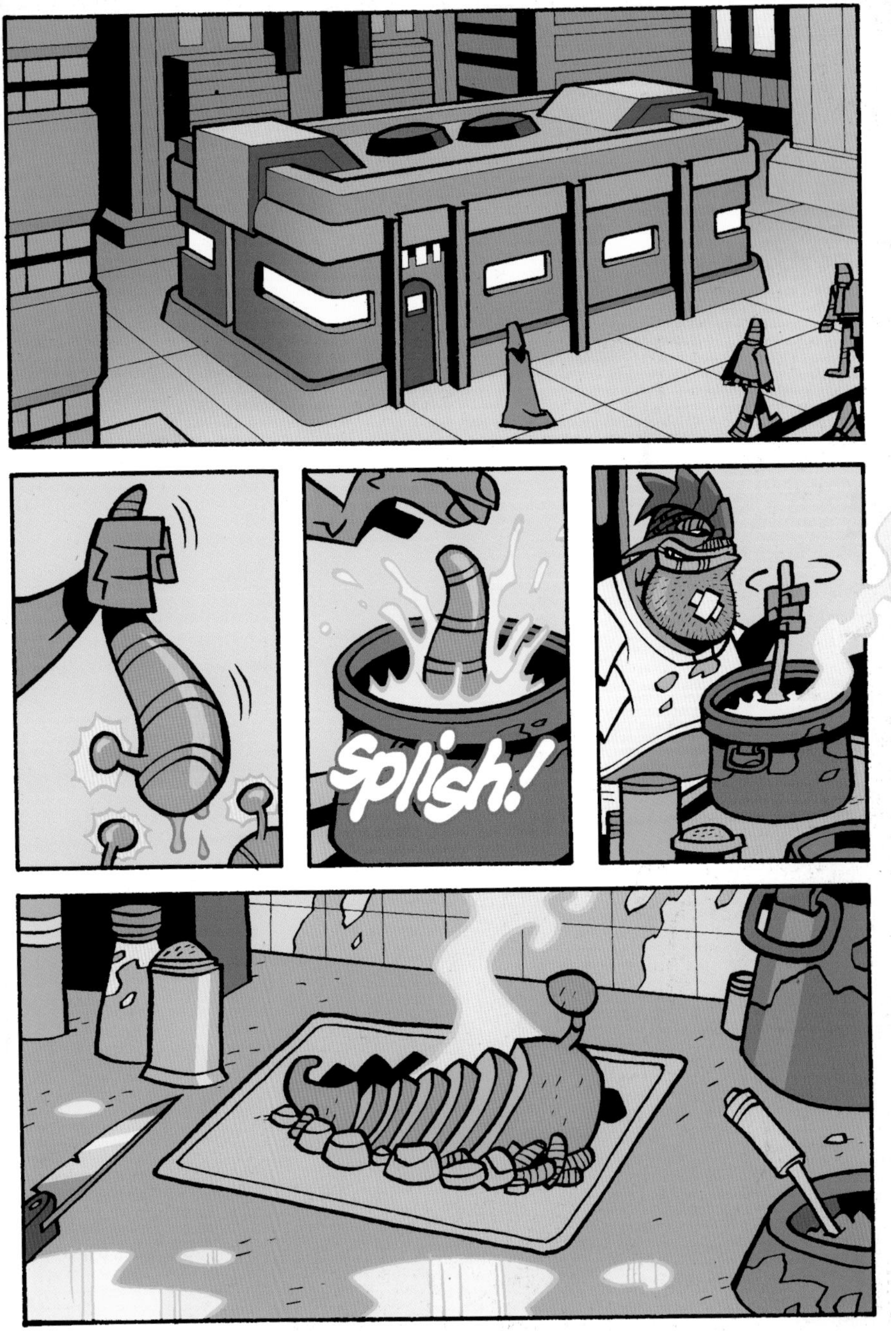
splish!

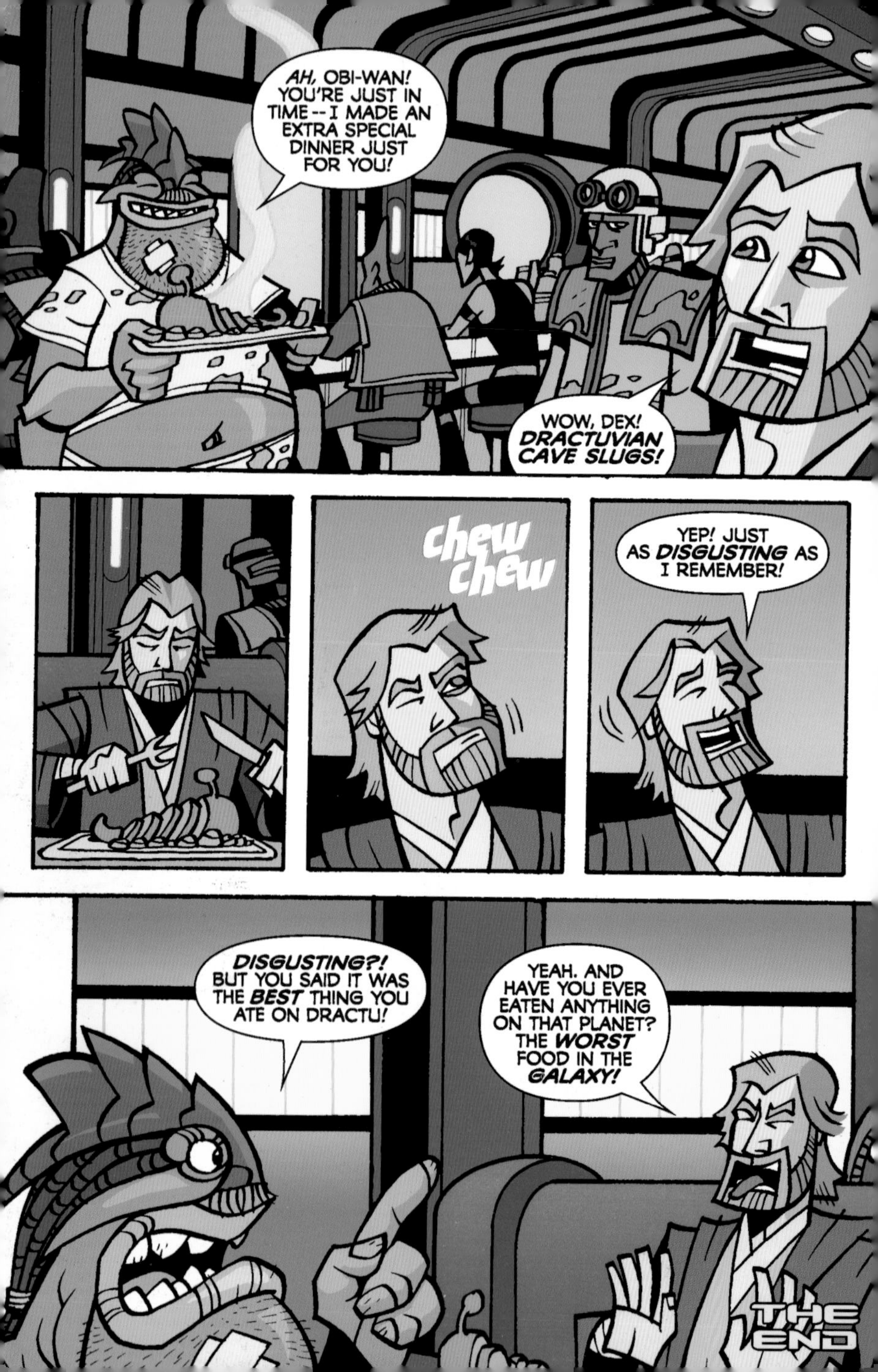
AH, OBI-WAN! YOU'RE JUST IN TIME -- I MADE AN EXTRA SPECIAL DINNER JUST FOR YOU!
WOW, DEX! DRACTUVIAN CAVE SLUGS!
chew chew
YEP! JUST AS DISGUSTING AS I REMEMBER!
DISGUSTING?! BUT YOU SAID IT WAS THE BEST THING YOU ATE ON DRACTU!
YEAH. AND HAVE YOU EVER EATEN ANYTHING ON THAT PLANET? THE WORST FOOD IN THE GALAXY!
THE END

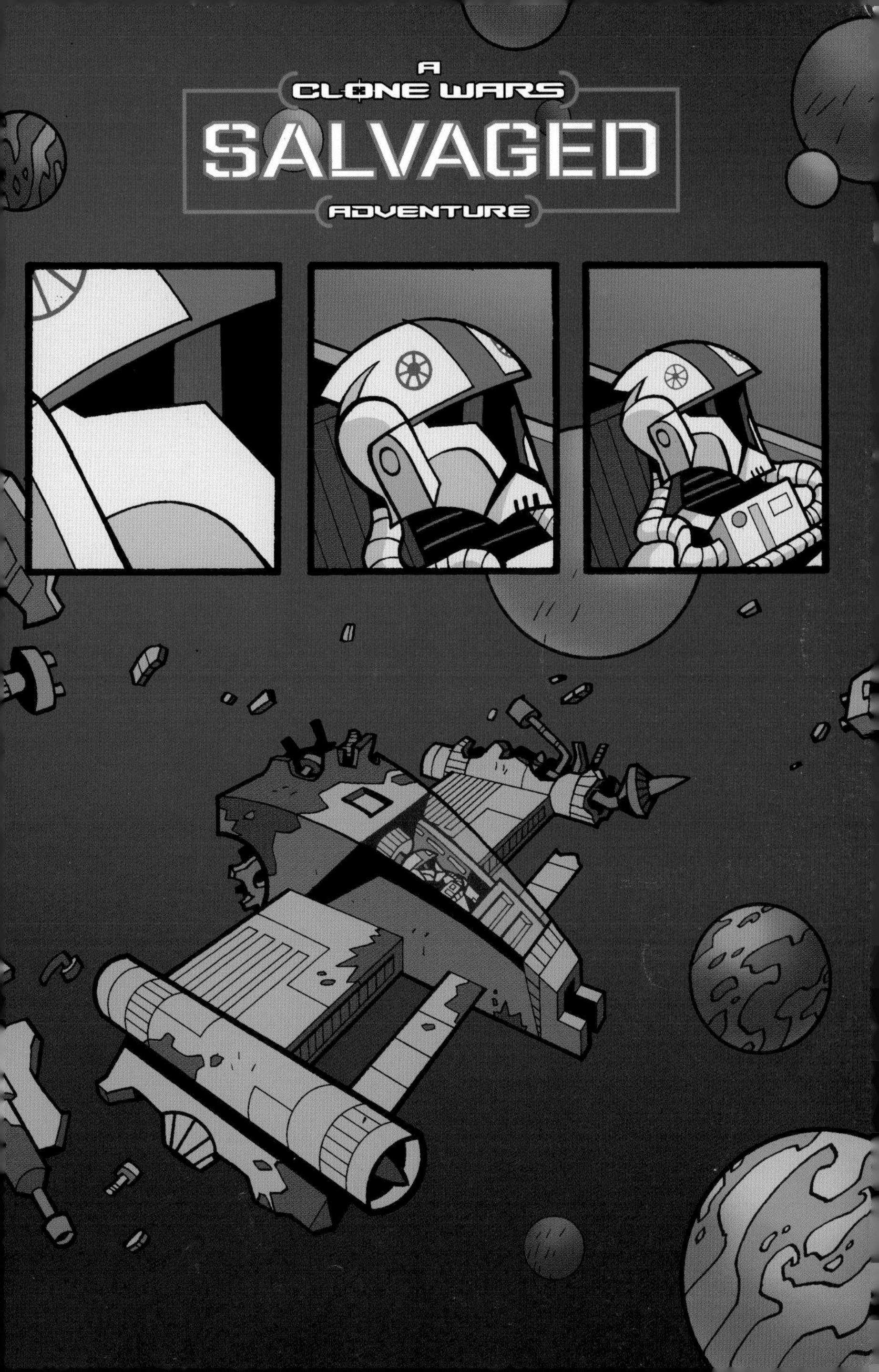
A
CLONE WARS
SALVAGED
ADVENTURE

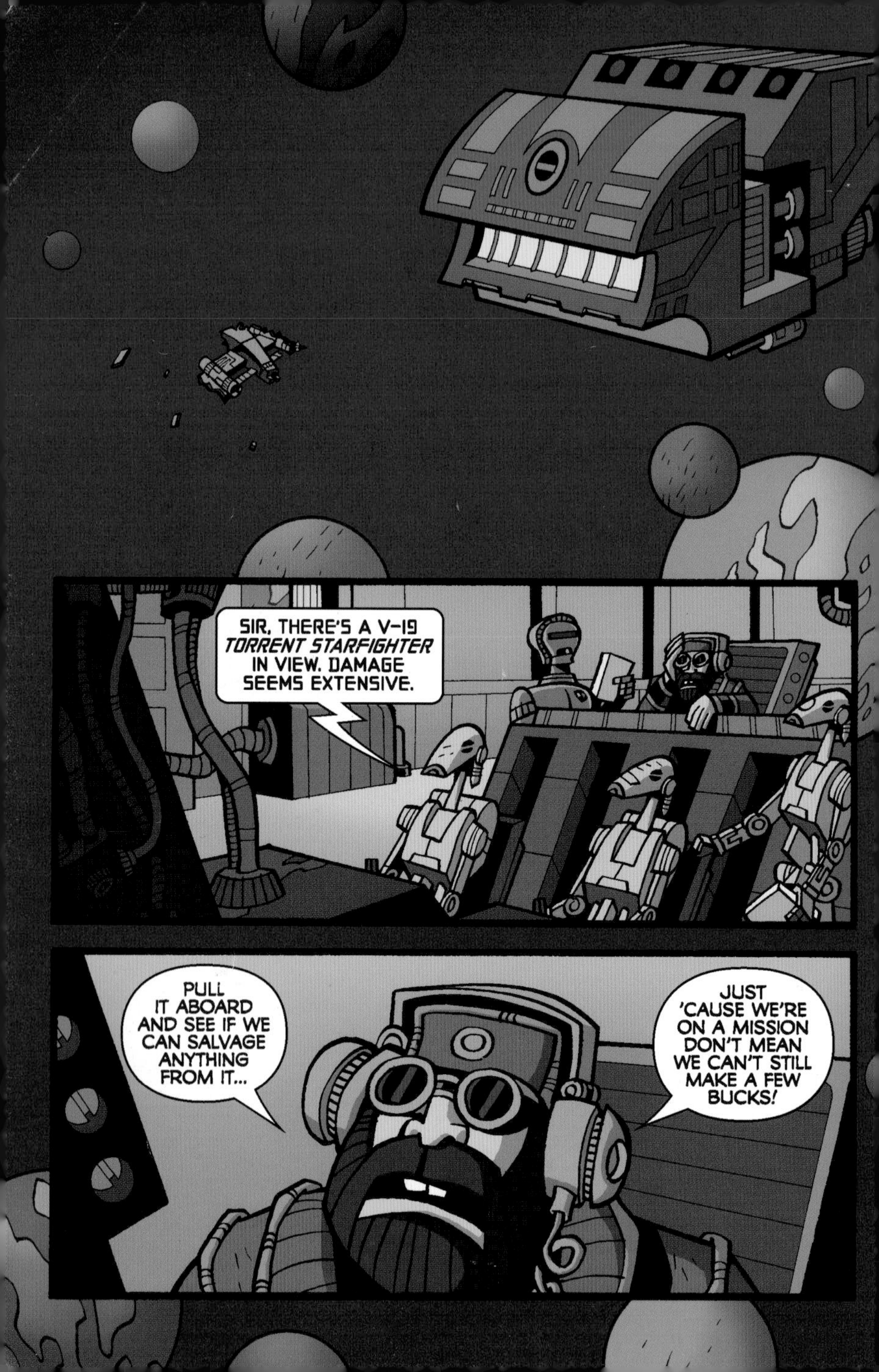
SIR, THERE'S A V-19 *TORRENT STARFIGHTER* IN VIEW. DAMAGE SEEMS EXTENSIVE.
PULL IT ABOARD AND SEE IF WE CAN SALVAGE ANYTHING FROM IT...
JUST 'CAUSE WE'RE ON A MISSION DON'T MEAN WE CAN'T STILL MAKE A FEW BUCKS!

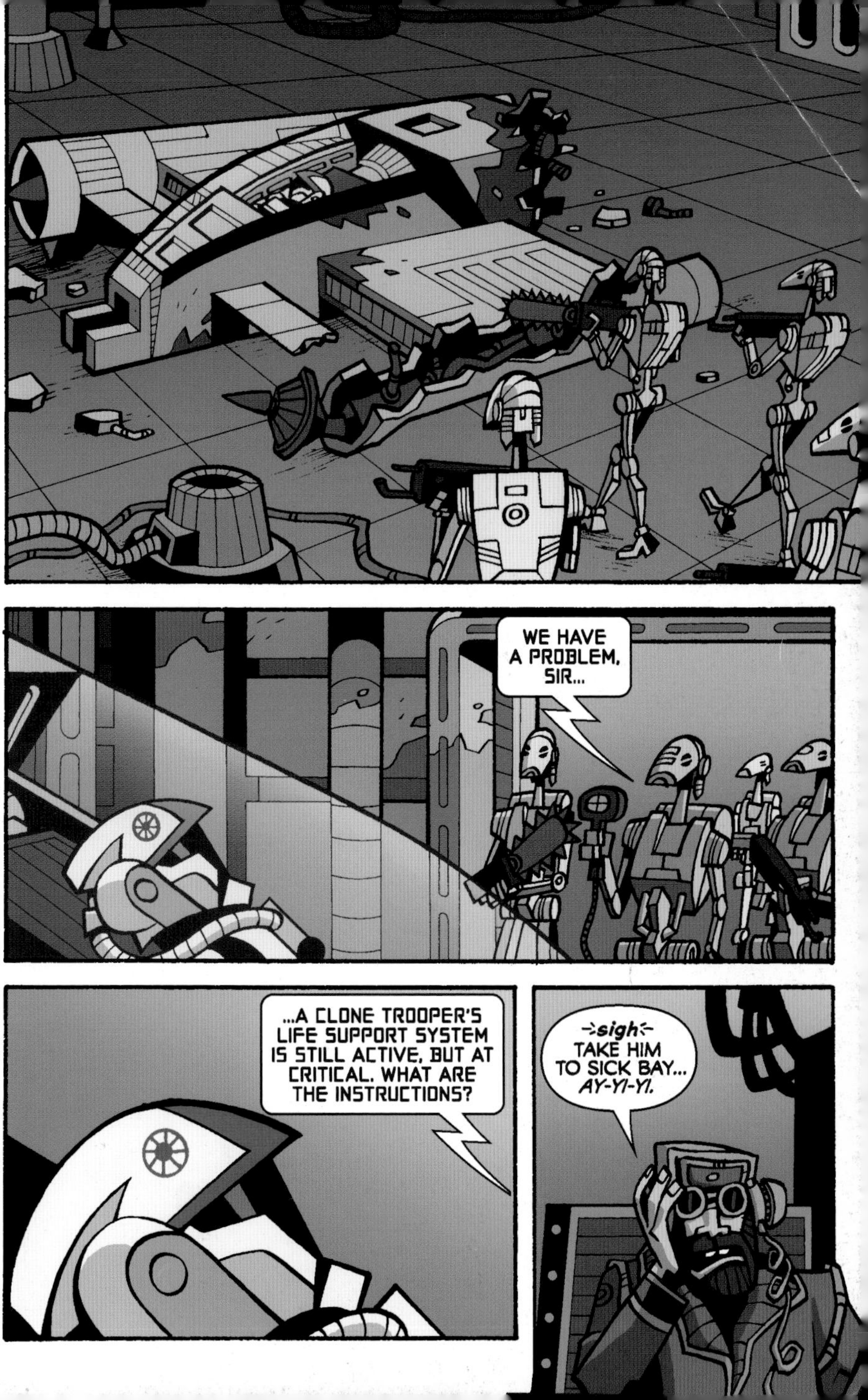
WE HAVE A PROBLEM, SIR...
...A CLONE TROOPER'S LIFE SUPPORT SYSTEM IS STILL ACTIVE, BUT AT CRITICAL. WHAT ARE THE INSTRUCTIONS?
-sigh- TAKE HIM TO SICK BAY... AY-YI-YI.

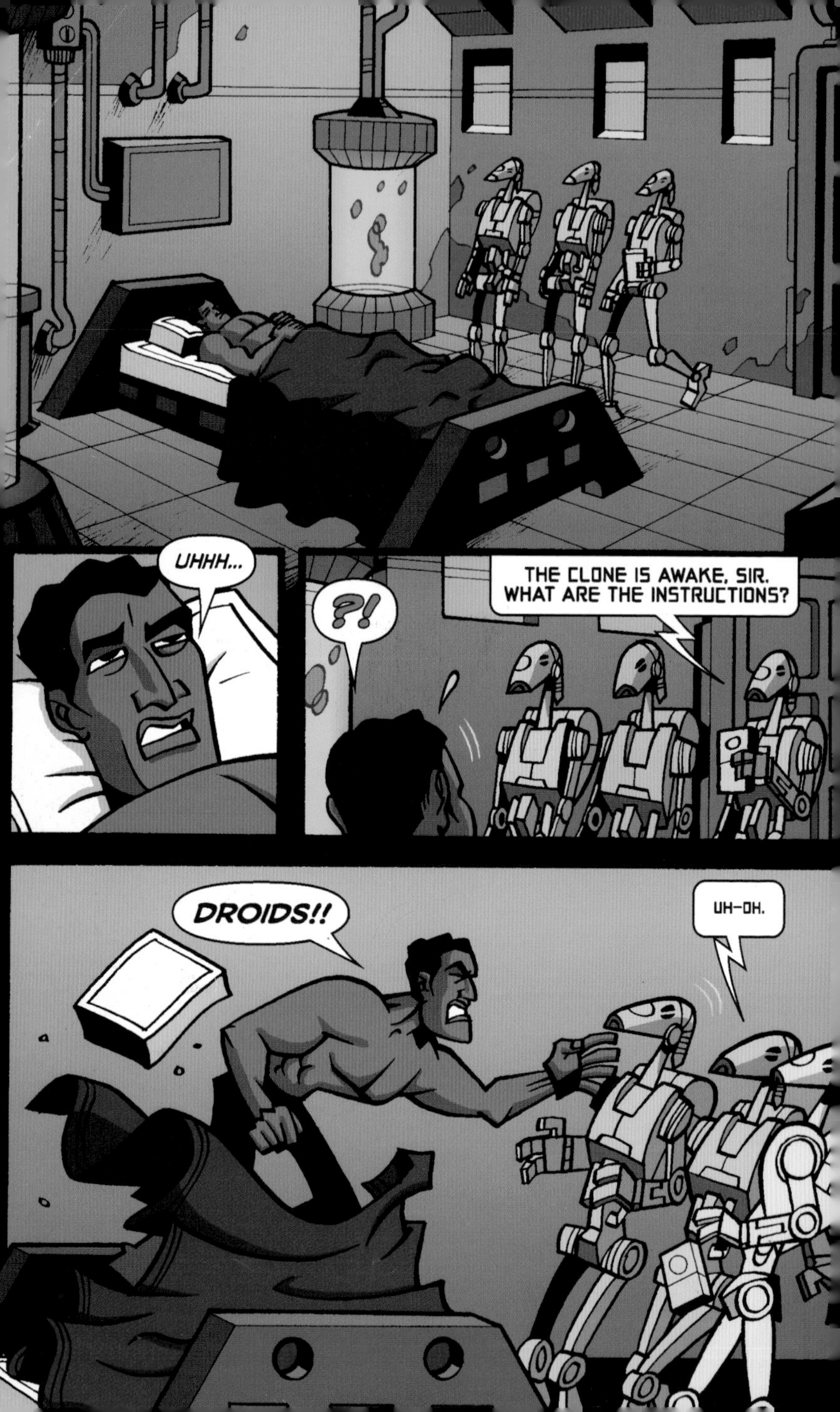
UHHH...
?!
THE CLONE IS AWAKE, SIR.
WHAT ARE THE INSTRUCTIONS?
DROIDS!!
UH-OH.

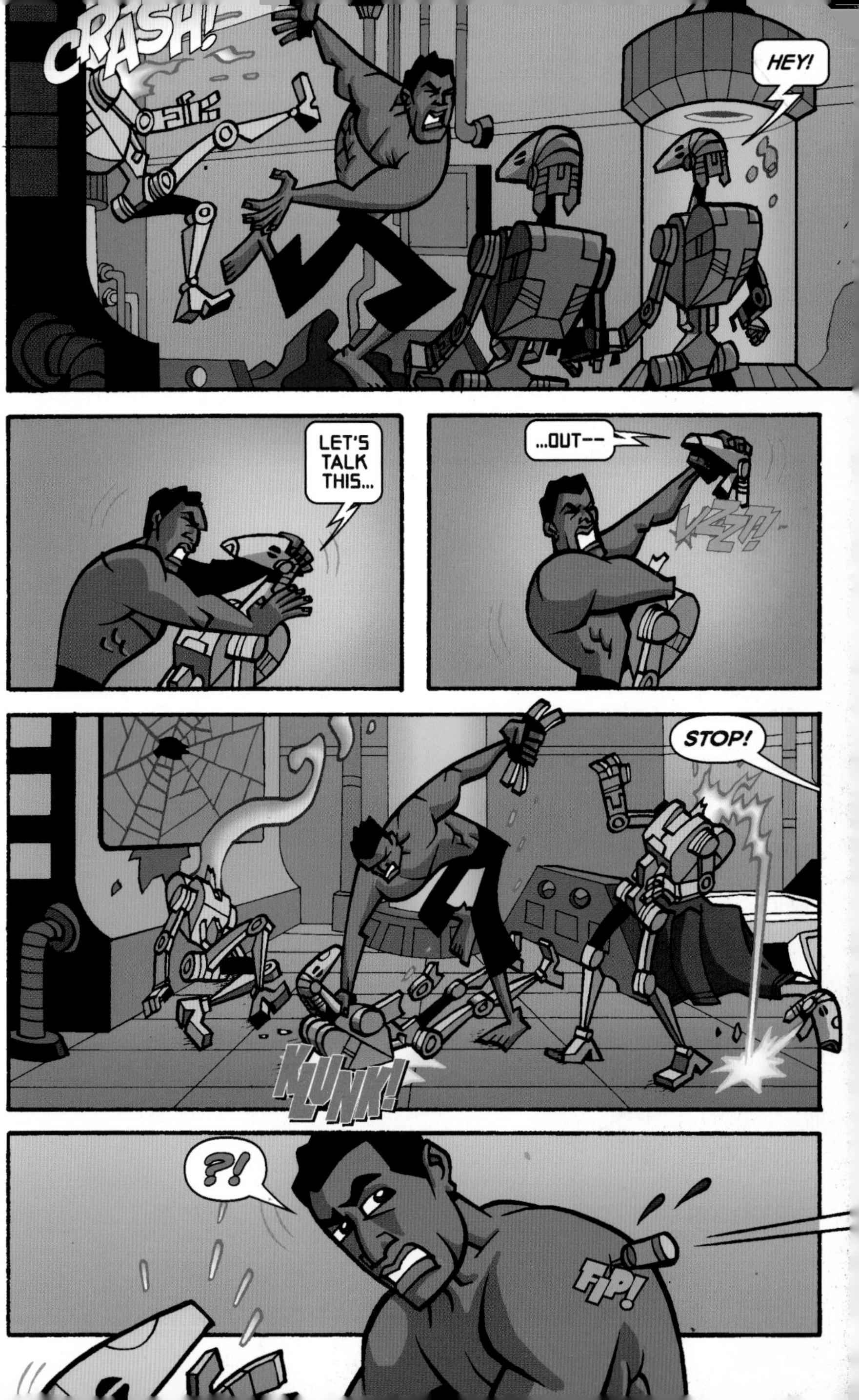
CRASH!
HEY!
LET'S TALK THIS...
...OUT--
VZZT!
STOP!
KLUNK!
?!
FIP!

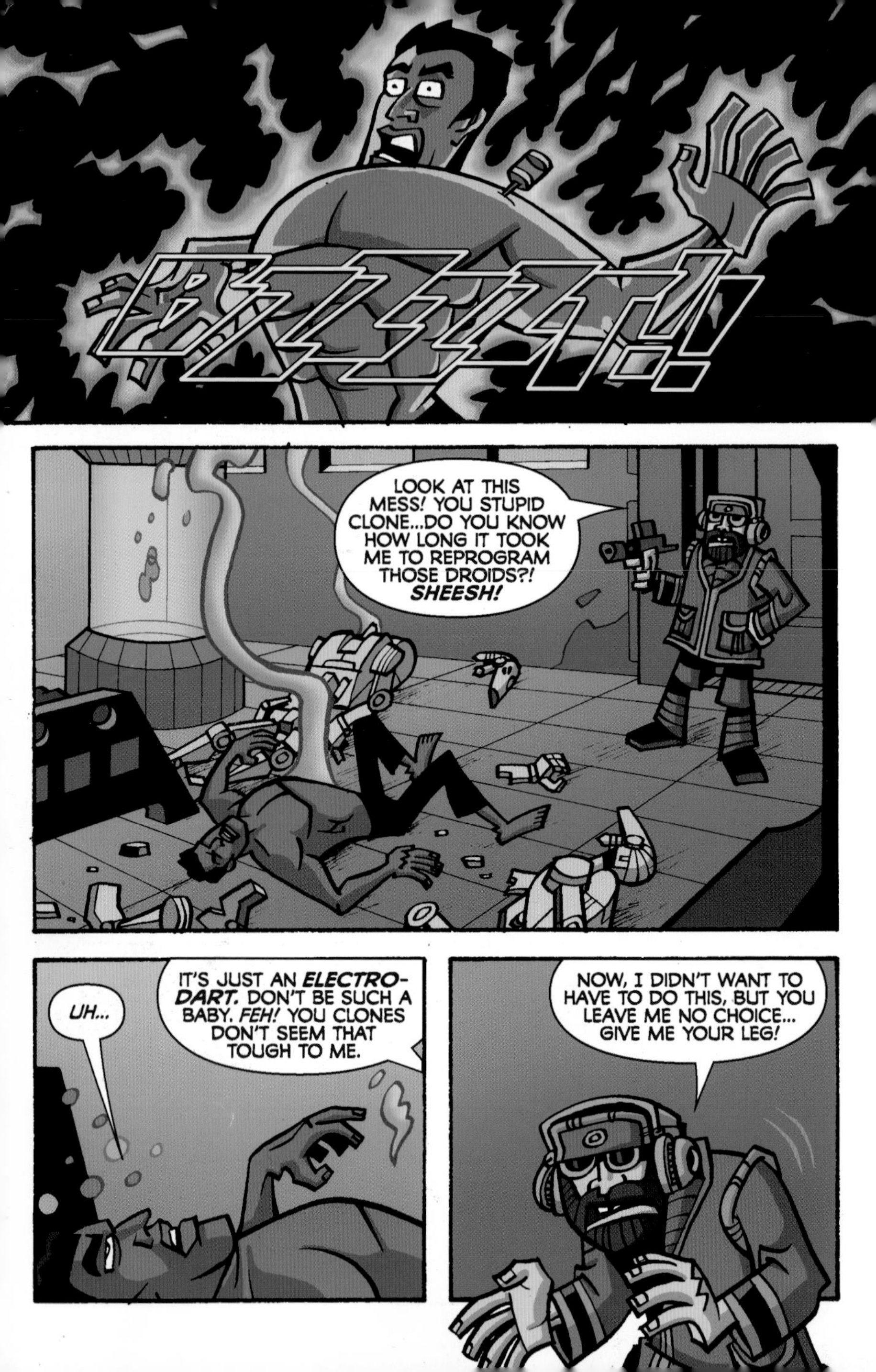
LOOK AT THIS MESS! YOU STUPID CLONE...DO YOU KNOW HOW LONG IT TOOK ME TO REPROGRAM THOSE DROIDS?! ***SHEESH!***
UH...
IT'S JUST AN ***ELECTRO-DART.*** DON'T BE SUCH A BABY. ***FEH!*** YOU CLONES DON'T SEEM THAT TOUGH TO ME.
NOW, I DIDN'T WANT TO HAVE TO DO THIS, BUT YOU LEAVE ME NO CHOICE... GIVE ME YOUR LEG!

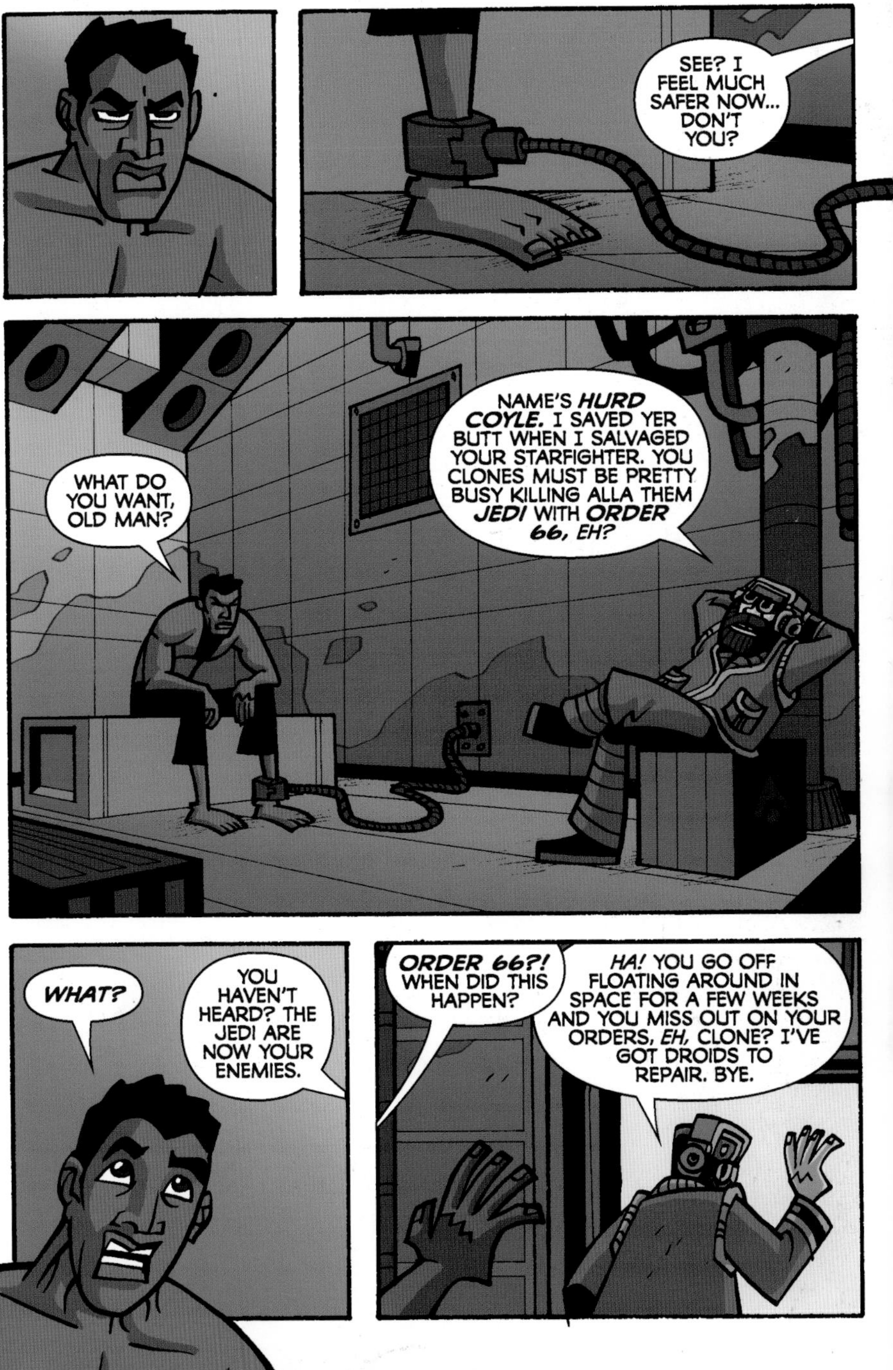

SEE? I FEEL MUCH SAFER NOW... DON'T YOU?
WHAT DO YOU WANT, OLD MAN?
NAME'S HURD COYLE. I SAVED YER BUTT WHEN I SALVAGED YOUR STARFIGHTER. YOU CLONES MUST BE PRETTY BUSY KILLING ALLA THEM JEDI WITH ORDER 66, EH?
WHAT?
YOU HAVEN'T HEARD? THE JEDI ARE NOW YOUR ENEMIES.
ORDER 66?! WHEN DID THIS HAPPEN?
HA! YOU GO OFF FLOATING AROUND IN SPACE FOR A FEW WEEKS AND YOU MISS OUT ON YOUR ORDERS, EH, CLONE? I'VE GOT DROIDS TO REPAIR. BYE.

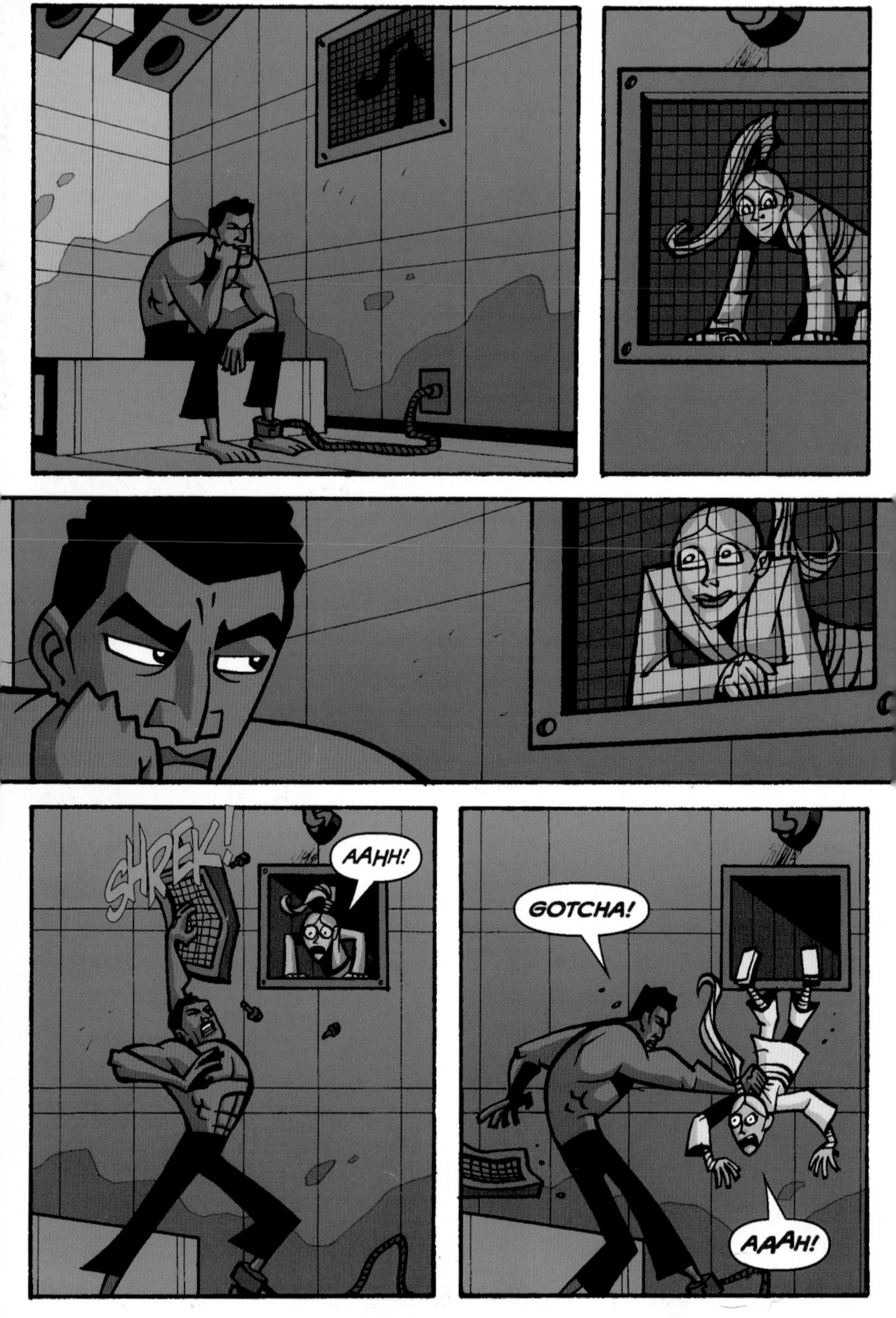
SHREK!
AAHH!
GOTCHA!
AAAH!

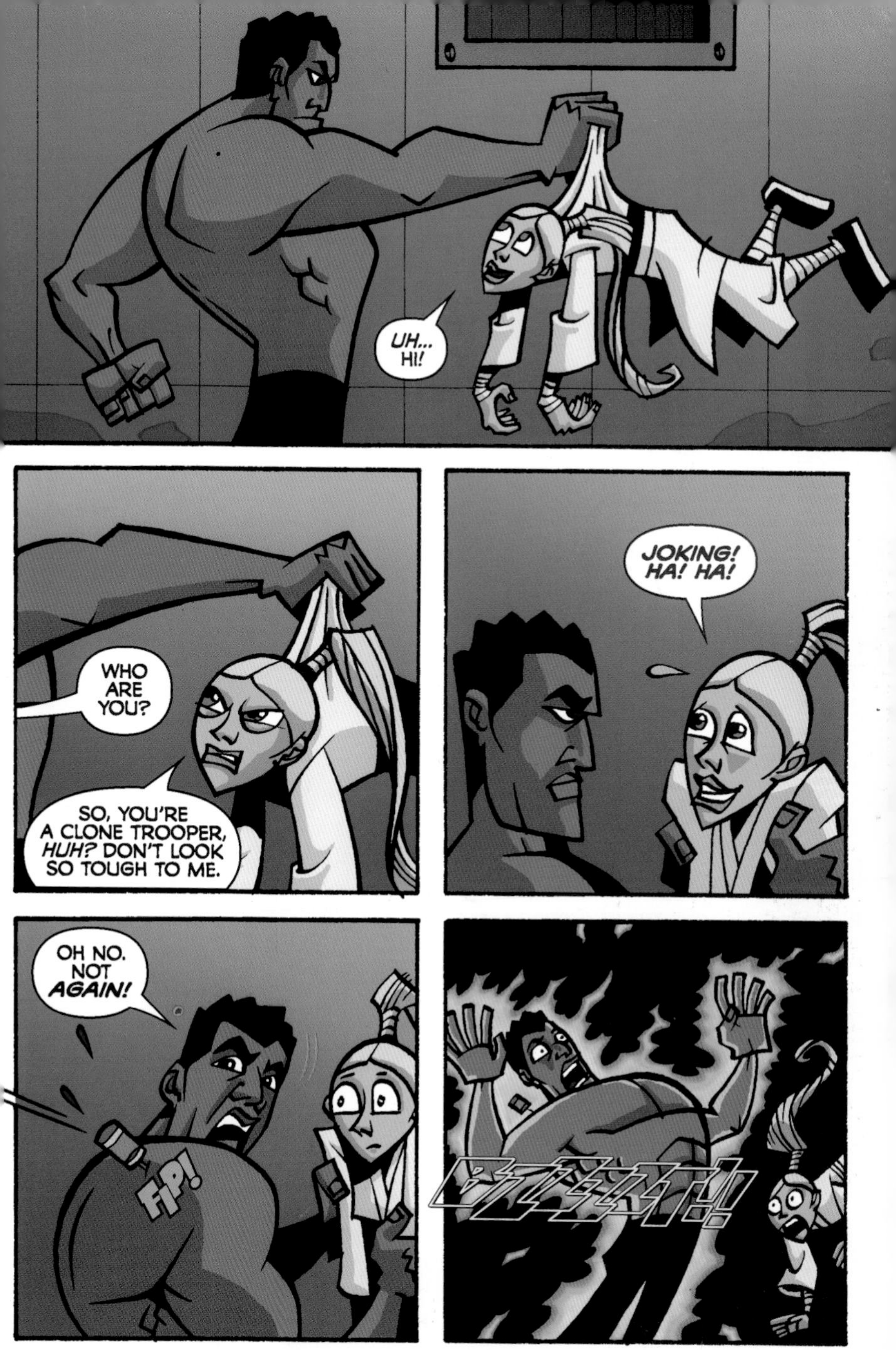
UH... HI!
WHO ARE YOU?
SO, YOU'RE A CLONE TROOPER, *HUH?* DON'T LOOK SO TOUGH TO ME.
JOKING! HA! HA!
OH NO. NOT *AGAIN!*
FIP!

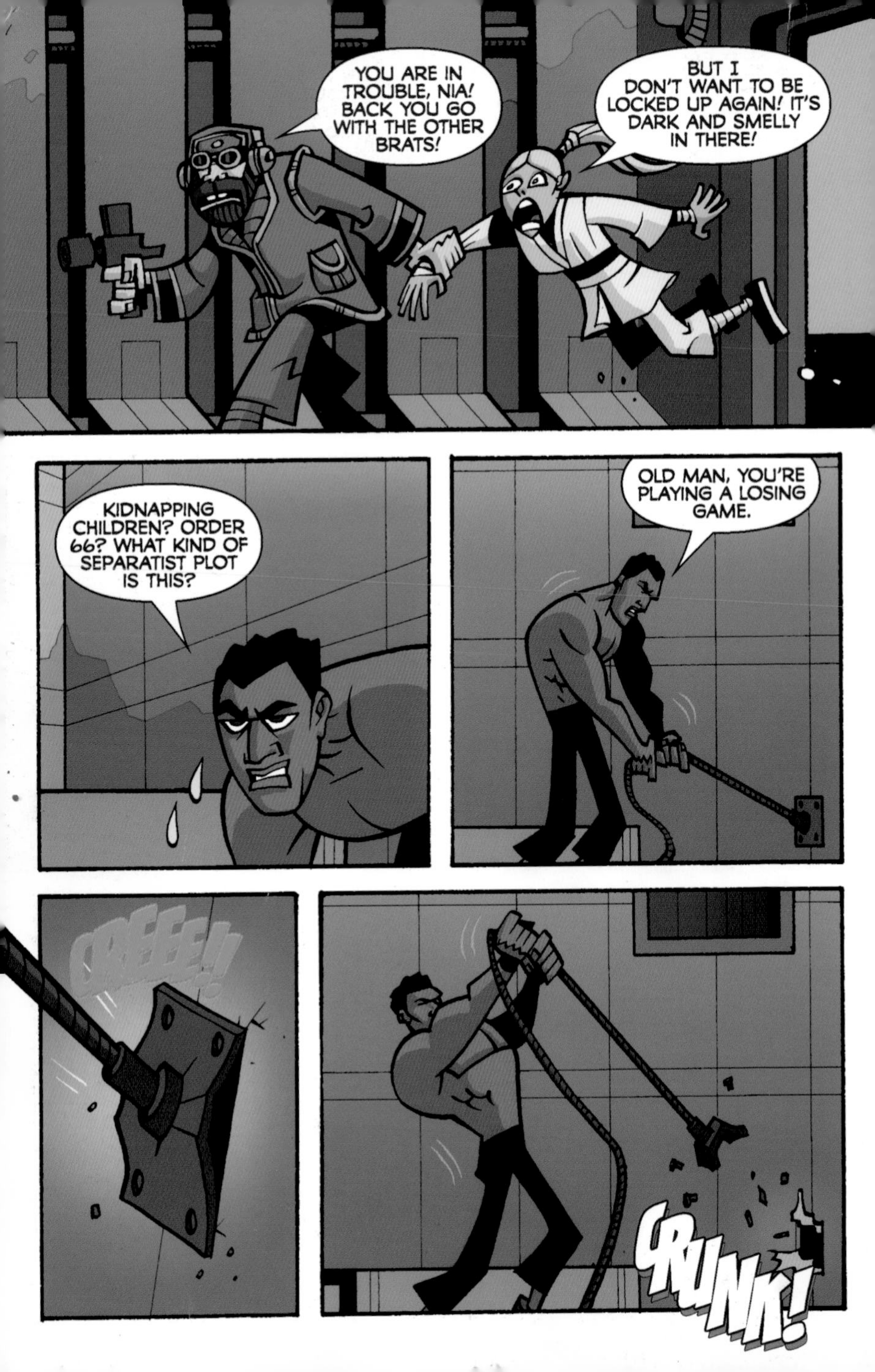
YOU ARE IN TROUBLE, NIA! BACK YOU GO WITH THE OTHER BRATS!
BUT I DON'T WANT TO BE LOCKED UP AGAIN! IT'S DARK AND SMELLY IN THERE!
KIDNAPPING CHILDREN? ORDER 66? WHAT KIND OF SEPARATIST PLOT IS THIS?
OLD MAN, YOU'RE PLAYING A LOSING GAME.
CREEE!!
CRUNK!

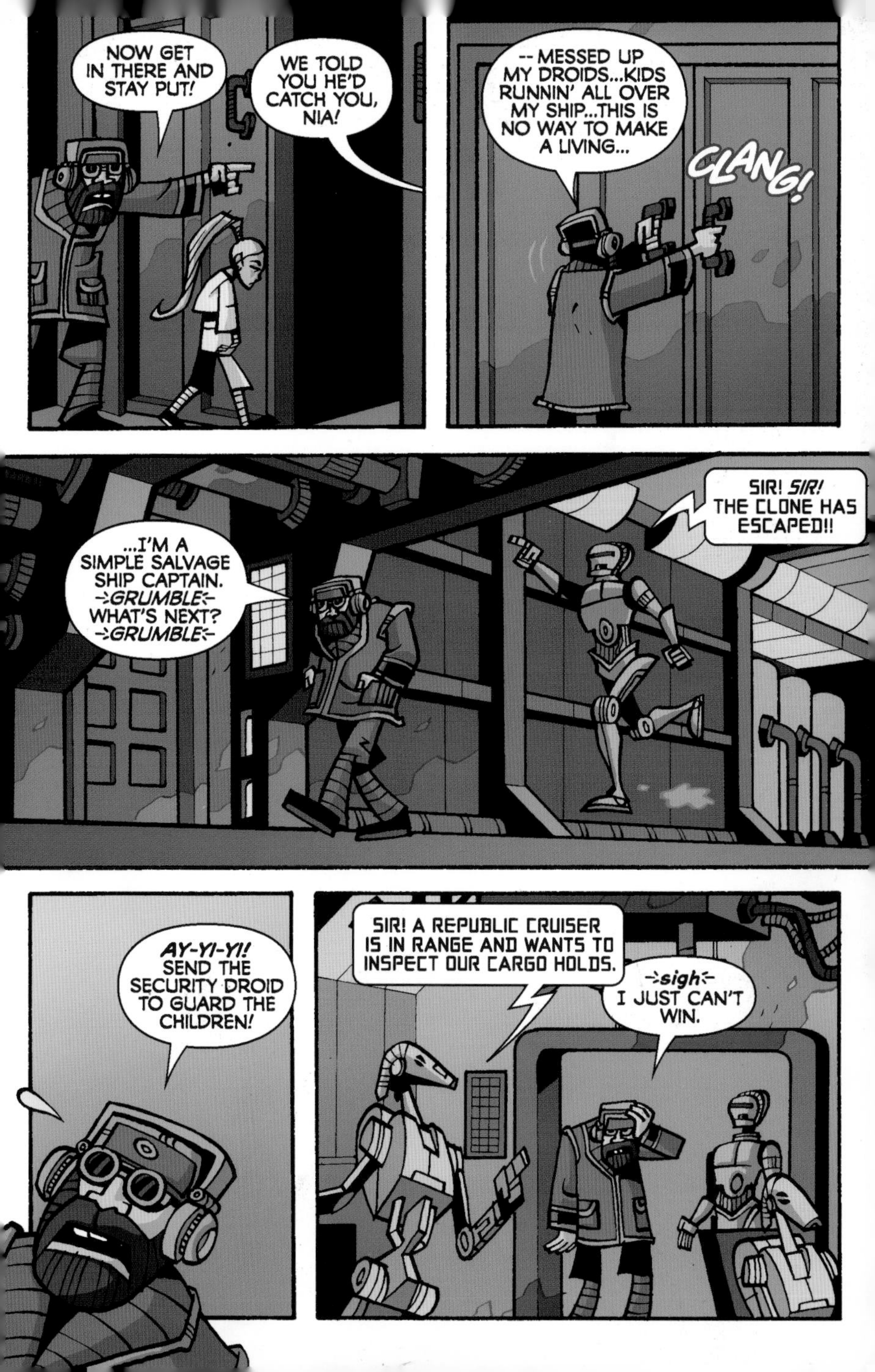

NOW GET IN THERE AND STAY PUT!
WE TOLD YOU HE'D CATCH YOU, NIA!
-- MESSED UP MY DROIDS...KIDS RUNNIN' ALL OVER MY SHIP...THIS IS NO WAY TO MAKE A LIVING...
CLANG!
...I'M A SIMPLE SALVAGE SHIP CAPTAIN. -GRUMBLE- WHAT'S NEXT? -GRUMBLE-
SIR! SIR! THE CLONE HAS ESCAPED!!
AY-YI-YI! SEND THE SECURITY DROID TO GUARD THE CHILDREN!
SIR! A REPUBLIC CRUISER IS IN RANGE AND WANTS TO INSPECT OUR CARGO HOLDS.
-sigh- I JUST CAN'T WIN.

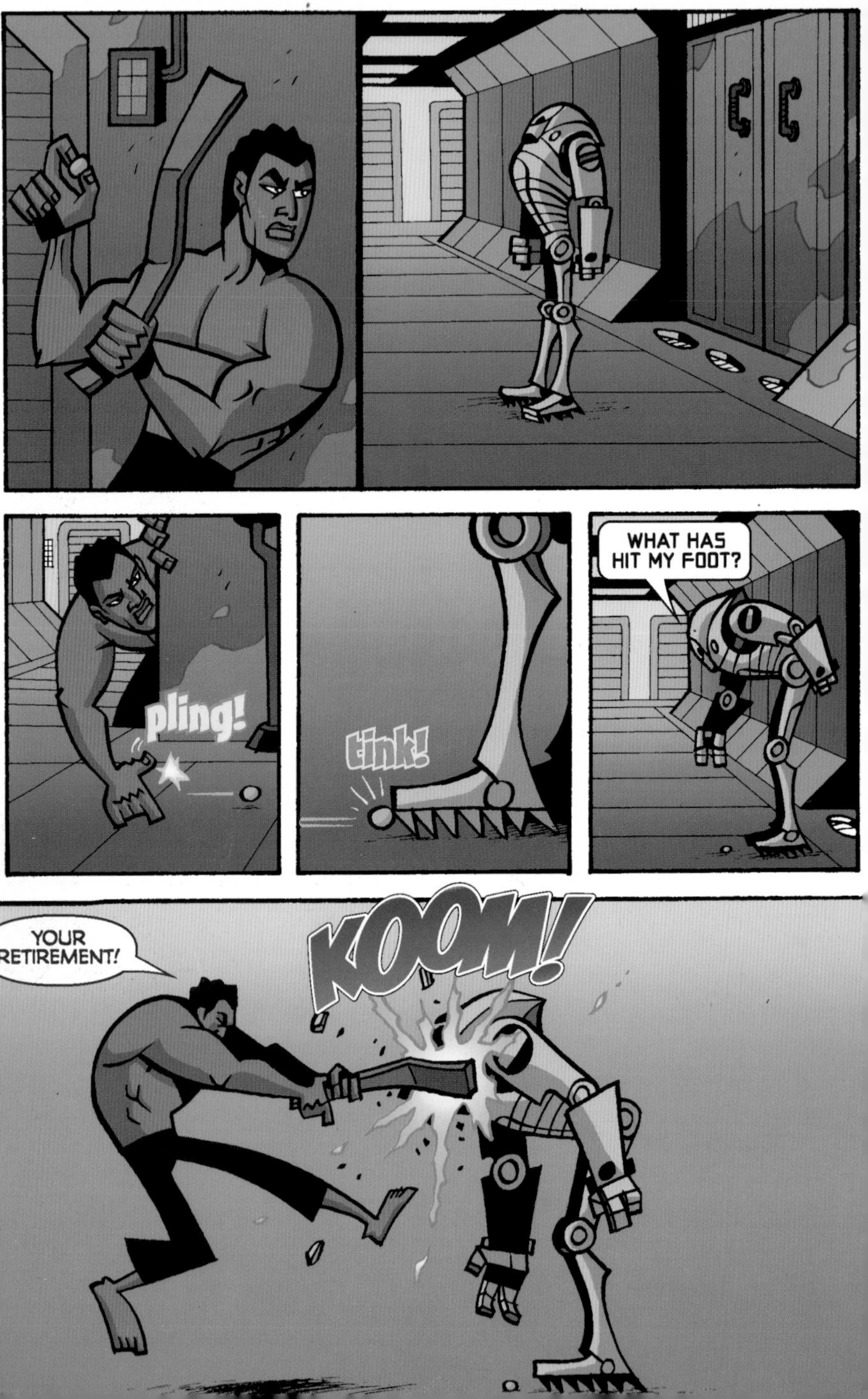

pling!
tink!
WHAT HAS HIT MY FOOT?
YOUR RETIREMENT!
KOOM!

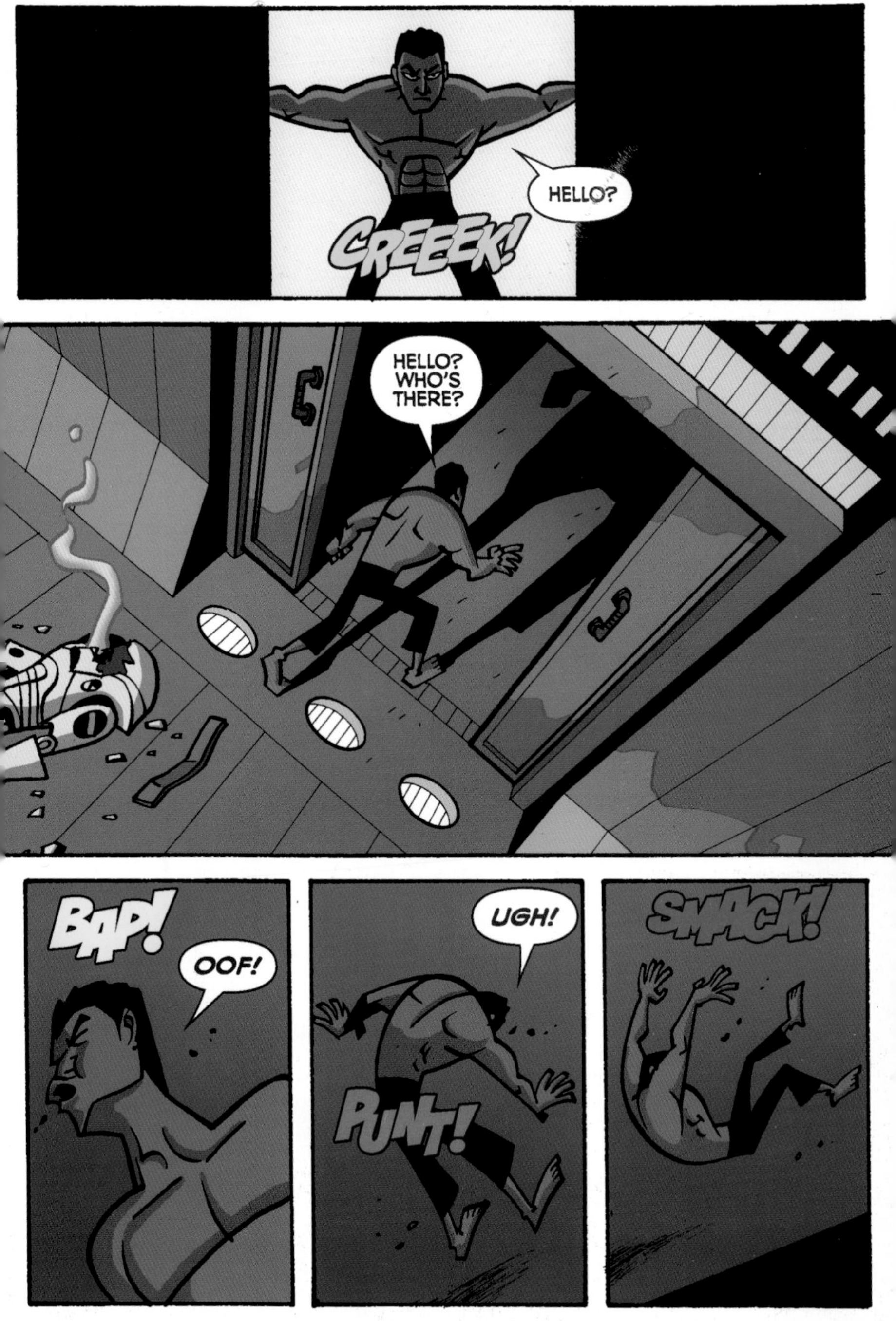
HELLO?
CREEEK!
HELLO? WHO'S THERE?
BAP!
OOF!
UGH!
PUNT!
SMACK!

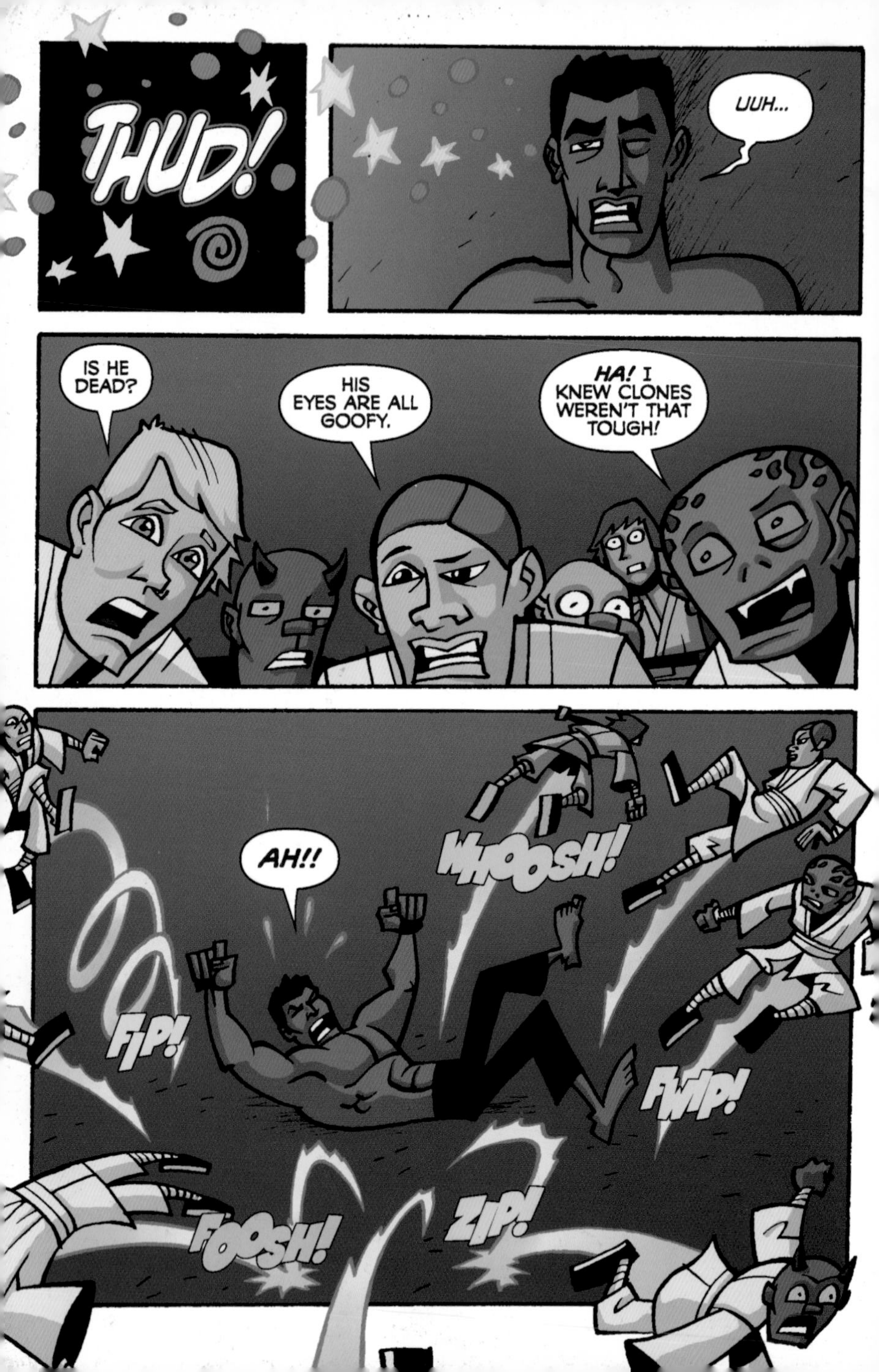
THUD!
UUH...
IS HE DEAD?
HIS EYES ARE ALL GOOFY.
HA! I KNEW CLONES WEREN'T THAT TOUGH!
AH!!
WHOOSH!
FIP!
FWIP!
FOOSH!
ZIP!

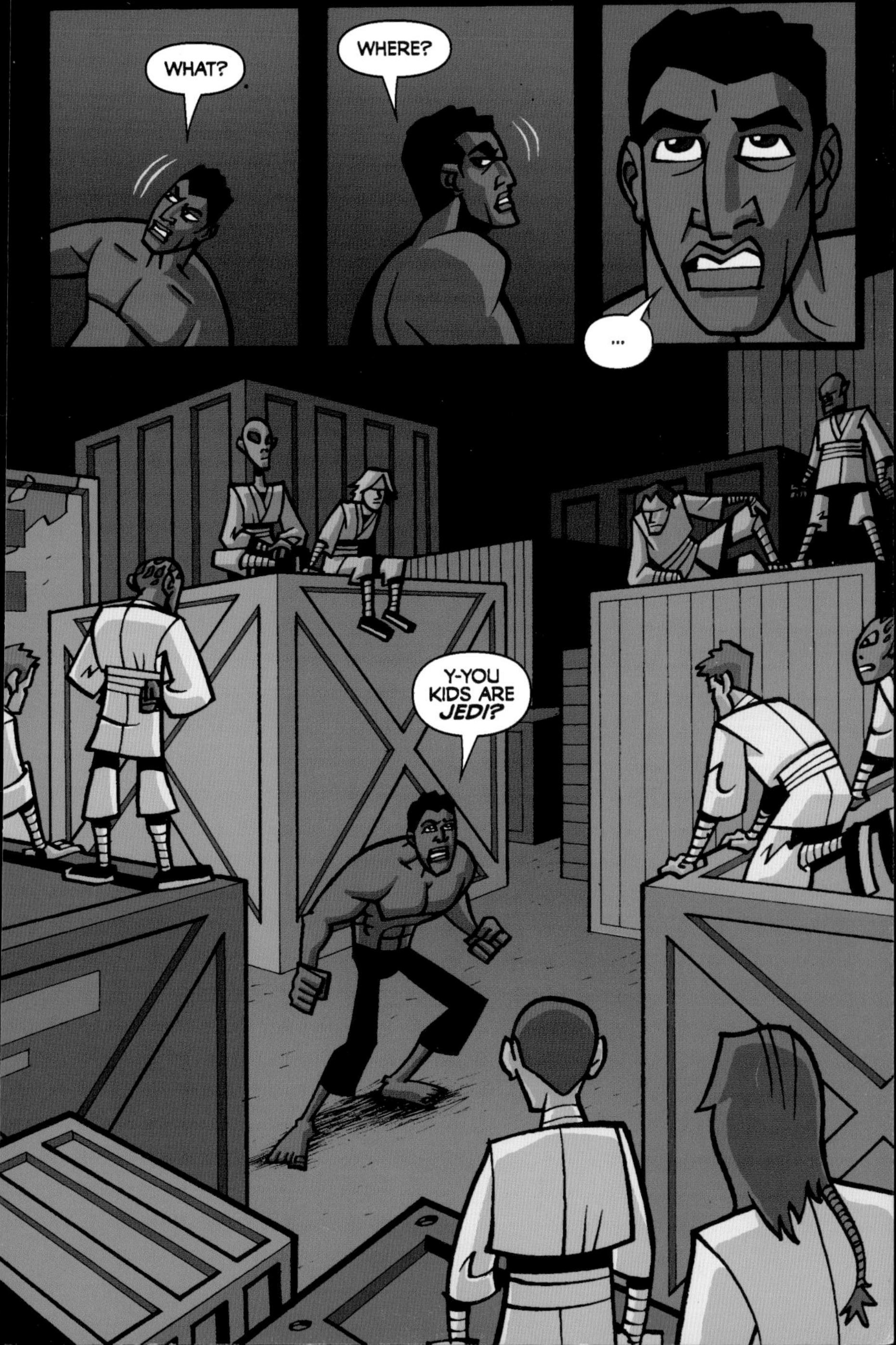
WHAT?
WHERE?
...
Y-YOU KIDS ARE *JEDI?*

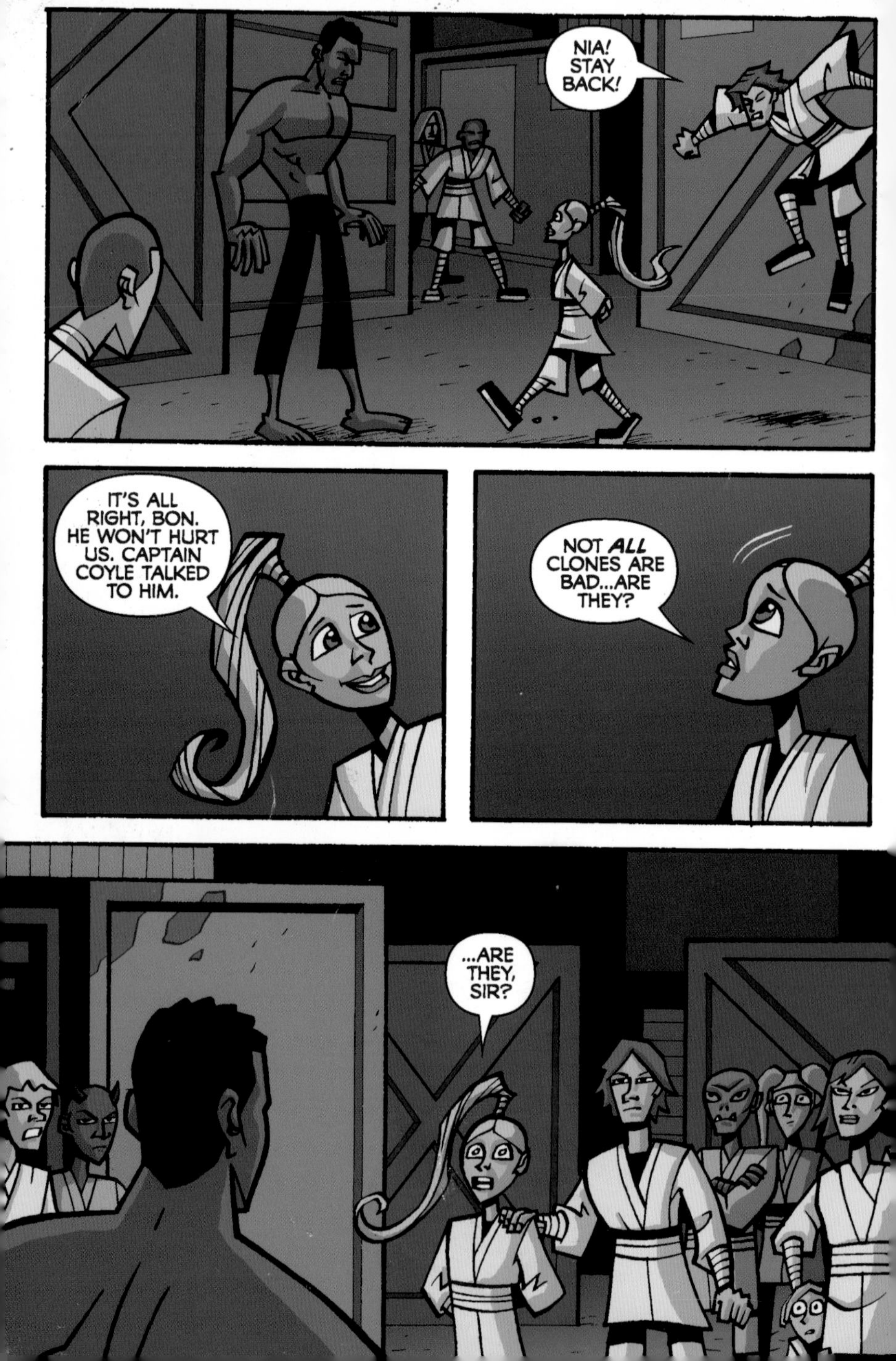
NIA! STAY BACK!
IT'S ALL RIGHT, BON. HE WON'T HURT US. CAPTAIN COYLE TALKED TO HIM.
NOT ALL CLONES ARE BAD...ARE THEY?
...ARE THEY, SIR?

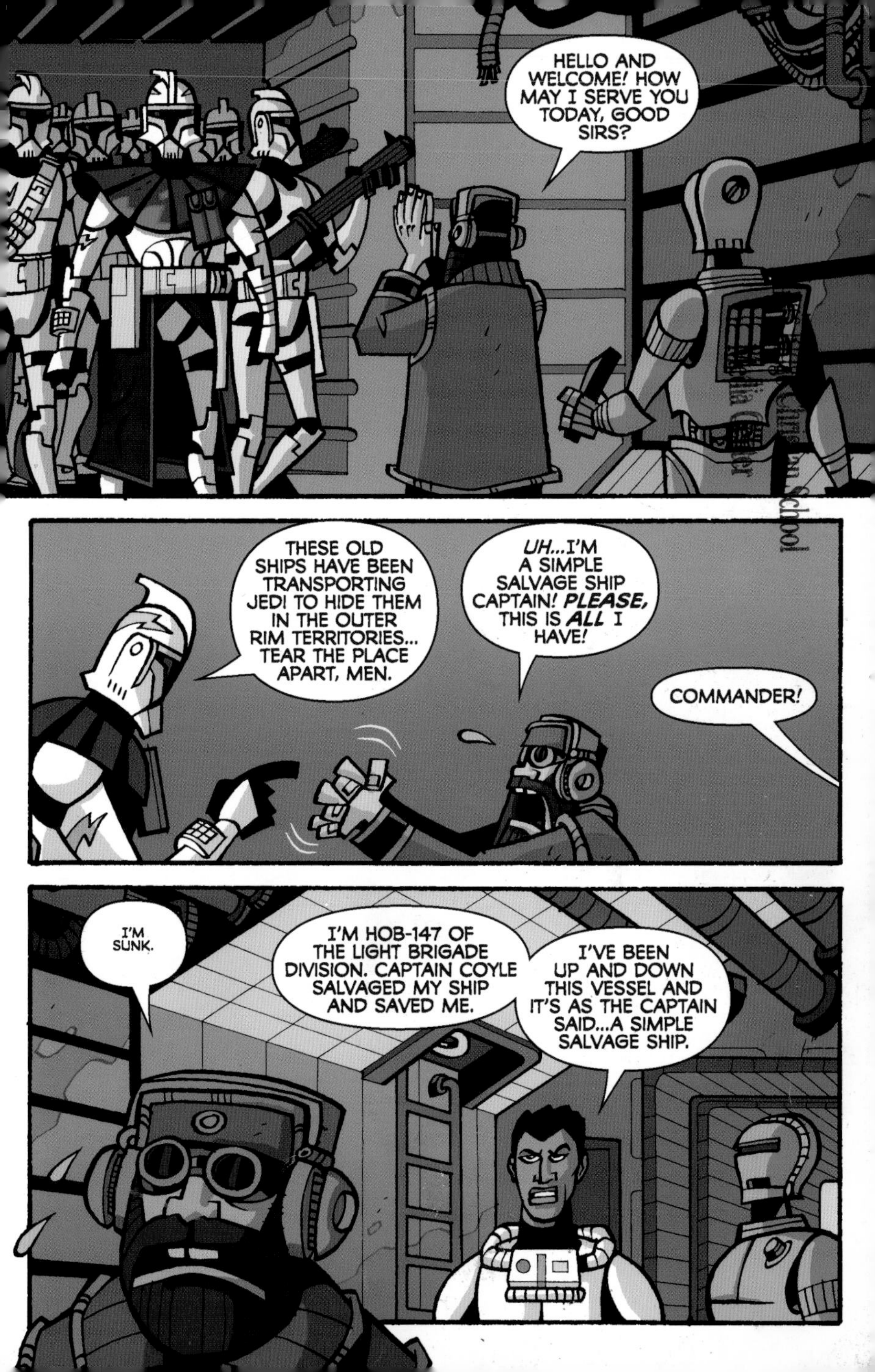
HELLO AND WELCOME! HOW MAY I SERVE YOU TODAY, GOOD SIRS?
THESE OLD SHIPS HAVE BEEN TRANSPORTING JEDI TO HIDE THEM IN THE OUTER RIM TERRITORIES... TEAR THE PLACE APART, MEN.
UH...I'M A SIMPLE SALVAGE SHIP CAPTAIN! ***PLEASE,*** THIS IS ***ALL*** I HAVE!
COMMANDER!
I'M SUNK.
I'M HOB-147 OF THE LIGHT BRIGADE DIVISION. CAPTAIN COYLE SALVAGED MY SHIP AND SAVED ME.
I'VE BEEN UP AND DOWN THIS VESSEL AND IT'S AS THE CAPTAIN SAID...A SIMPLE SALVAGE SHIP.

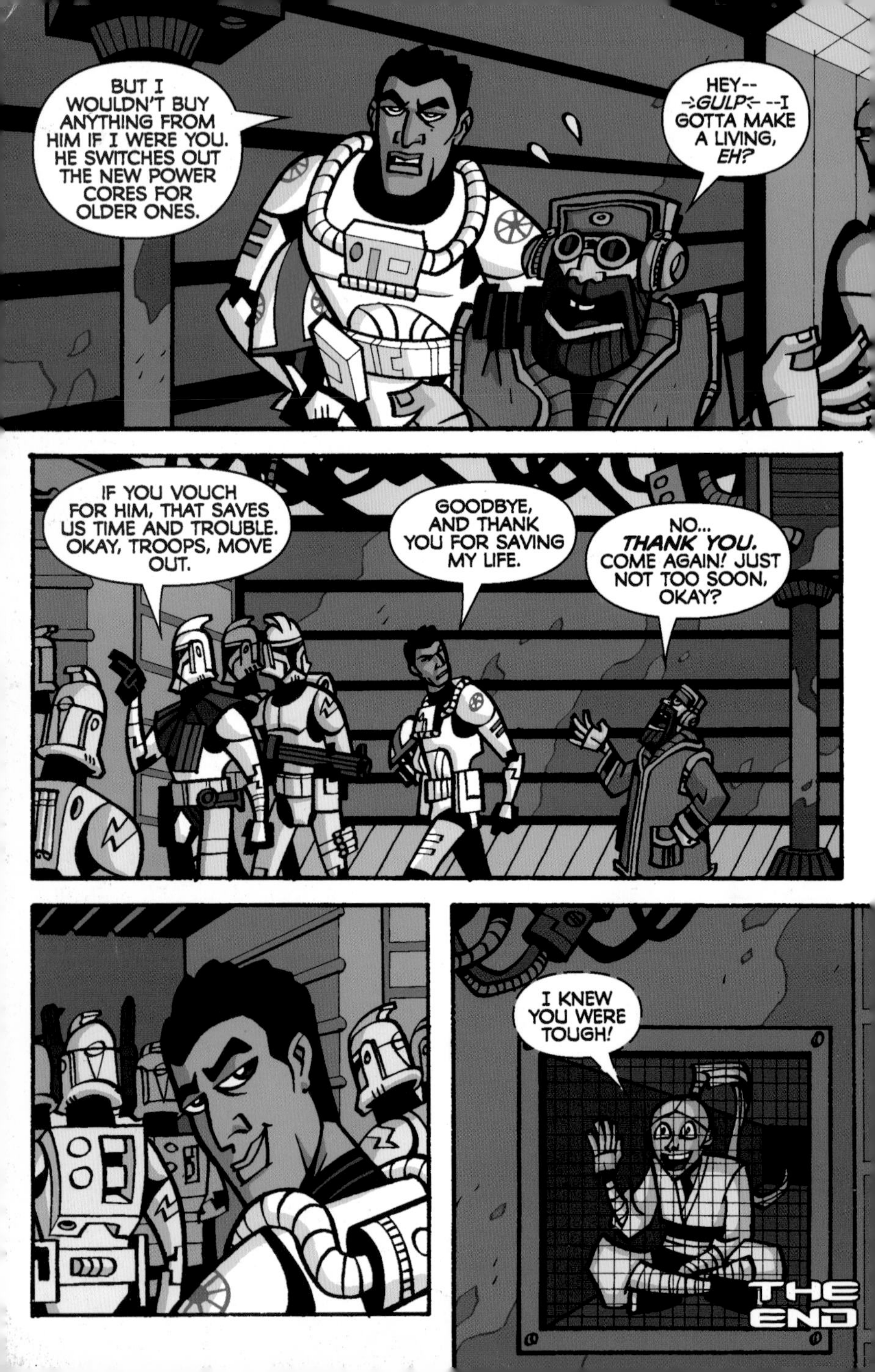
BUT I WOULDN'T BUY ANYTHING FROM HIM IF I WERE YOU. HE SWITCHES OUT THE NEW POWER CORES FOR OLDER ONES.
HEY-- -›GULP‹- --I GOTTA MAKE A LIVING, EH?
IF YOU VOUCH FOR HIM, THAT SAVES US TIME AND TROUBLE. OKAY, TROOPS, MOVE OUT.
GOODBYE, AND THANK YOU FOR SAVING MY LIFE.
NO... THANK YOU. COME AGAIN! JUST NOT TOO SOON, OKAY?
I KNEW YOU WERE TOUGH!
THE END

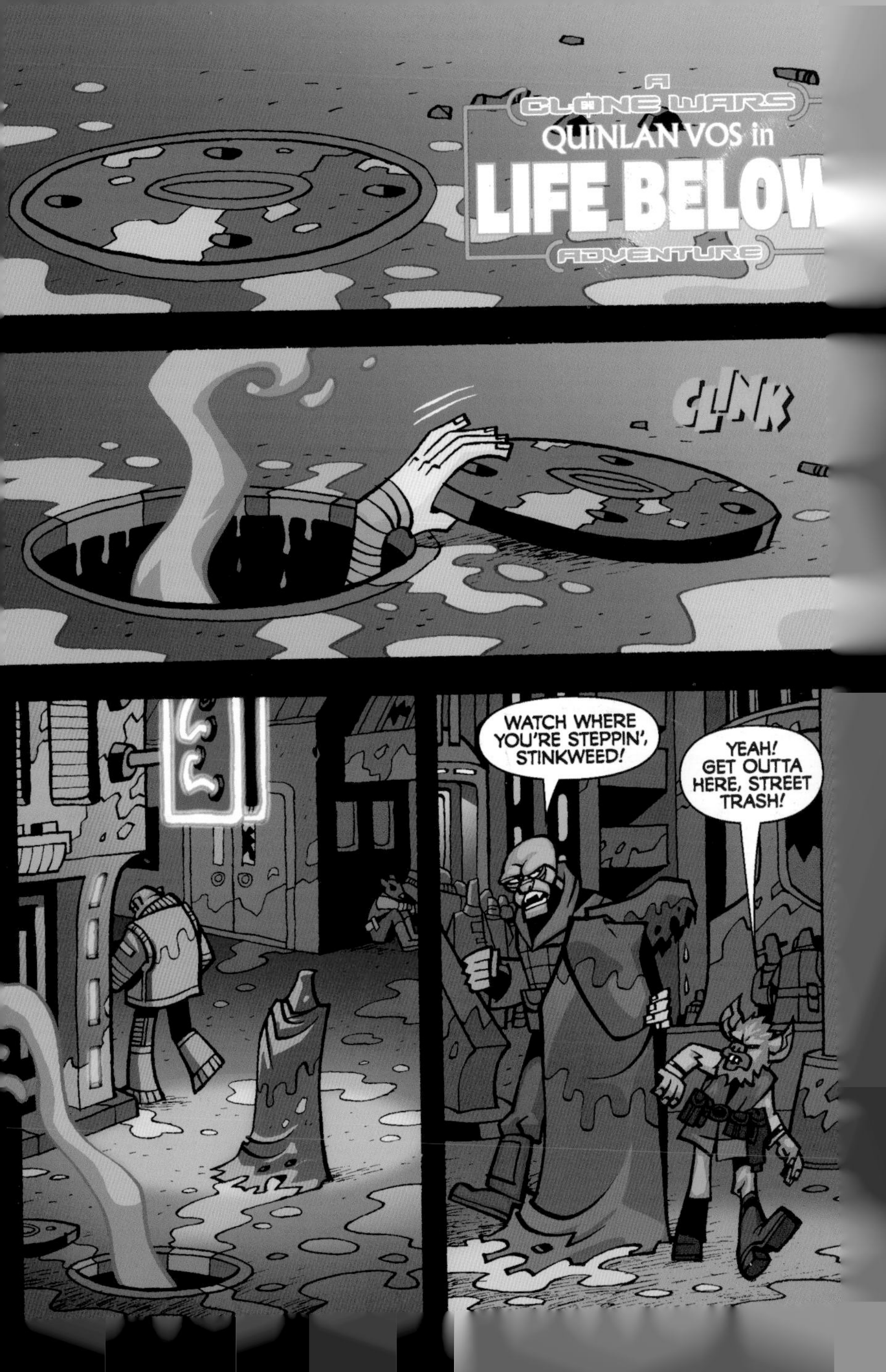
A CLONE WARS
QUINLAN VOS in
LIFE BELOW
ADVENTURE
CLINK
WATCH WHERE YOU'RE STEPPIN', STINKWEED!
YEAH! GET OUTTA HERE, STREET TRASH!

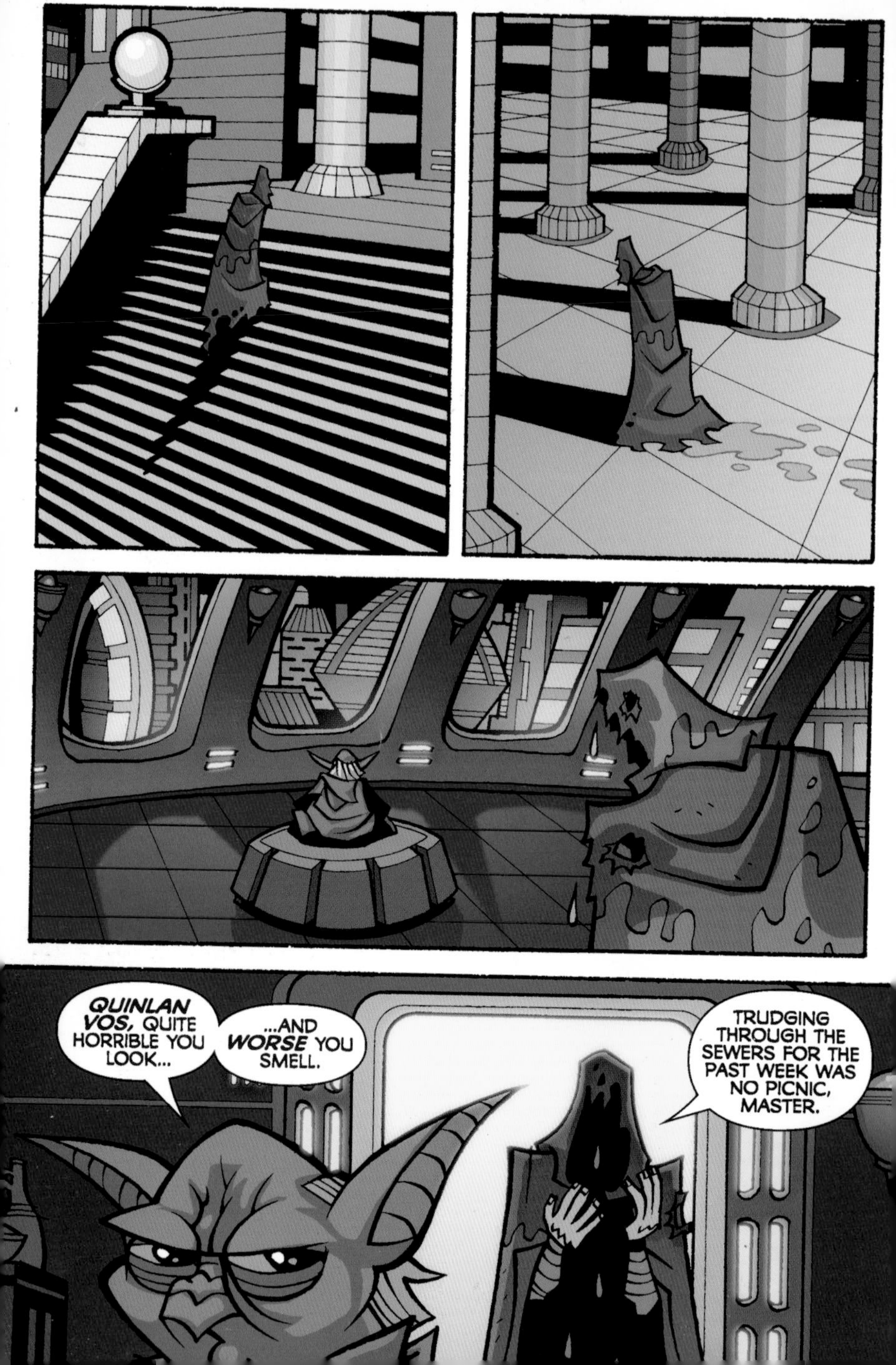
QUINLAN VOS, QUITE HORRIBLE YOU LOOK...
...AND WORSE YOU SMELL.
TRUDGING THROUGH THE SEWERS FOR THE PAST WEEK WAS NO PICNIC, MASTER.

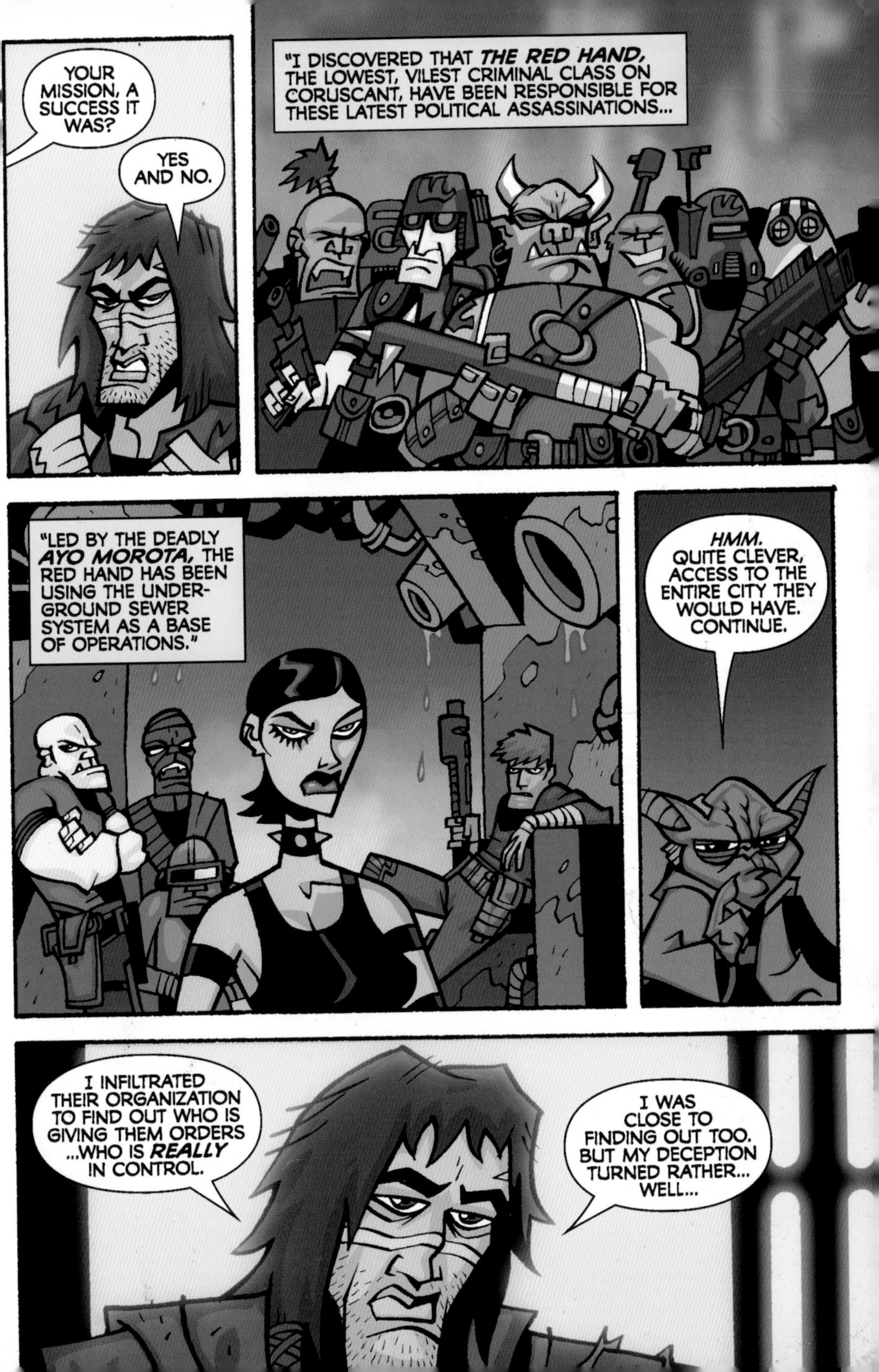
YOUR MISSION, A SUCCESS IT WAS?
YES AND NO.
"I DISCOVERED THAT *THE RED HAND,* THE LOWEST, VILEST CRIMINAL CLASS ON CORUSCANT, HAVE BEEN RESPONSIBLE FOR THESE LATEST POLITICAL ASSASSINATIONS...
"LED BY THE DEADLY *AYO MOROTA,* THE RED HAND HAS BEEN USING THE UNDER-GROUND SEWER SYSTEM AS A BASE OF OPERATIONS."
HMM. QUITE CLEVER, ACCESS TO THE ENTIRE CITY THEY WOULD HAVE. CONTINUE.
I INFILTRATED THEIR ORGANIZATION TO FIND OUT WHO IS GIVING THEM ORDERS ...WHO IS *REALLY* IN CONTROL.
I WAS CLOSE TO FINDING OUT TOO. BUT MY DECEPTION TURNED RATHER... WELL...

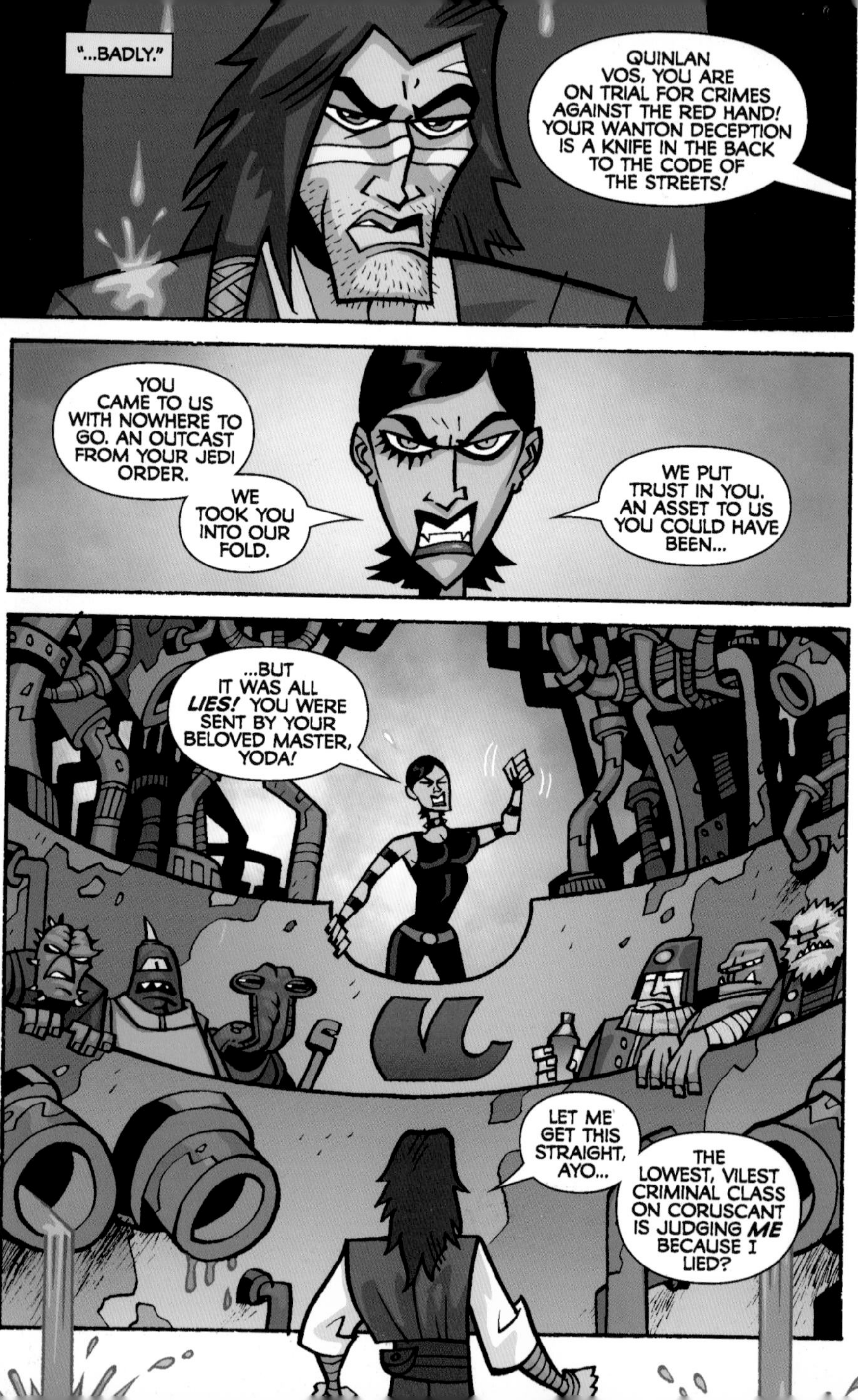
"...BADLY."
QUINLAN VOS, YOU ARE ON TRIAL FOR CRIMES AGAINST THE RED HAND! YOUR WANTON DECEPTION IS A KNIFE IN THE BACK TO THE CODE OF THE STREETS!
YOU CAME TO US WITH NOWHERE TO GO. AN OUTCAST FROM YOUR JEDI ORDER.
WE TOOK YOU INTO OUR FOLD.
WE PUT TRUST IN YOU. AN ASSET TO US YOU COULD HAVE BEEN...
...BUT IT WAS ALL *LIES!* YOU WERE SENT BY YOUR BELOVED MASTER, YODA!
LET ME GET THIS STRAIGHT, AYO...
THE LOWEST, VILEST CRIMINAL CLASS ON CORUSCANT IS JUDGING *ME* BECAUSE I LIED?

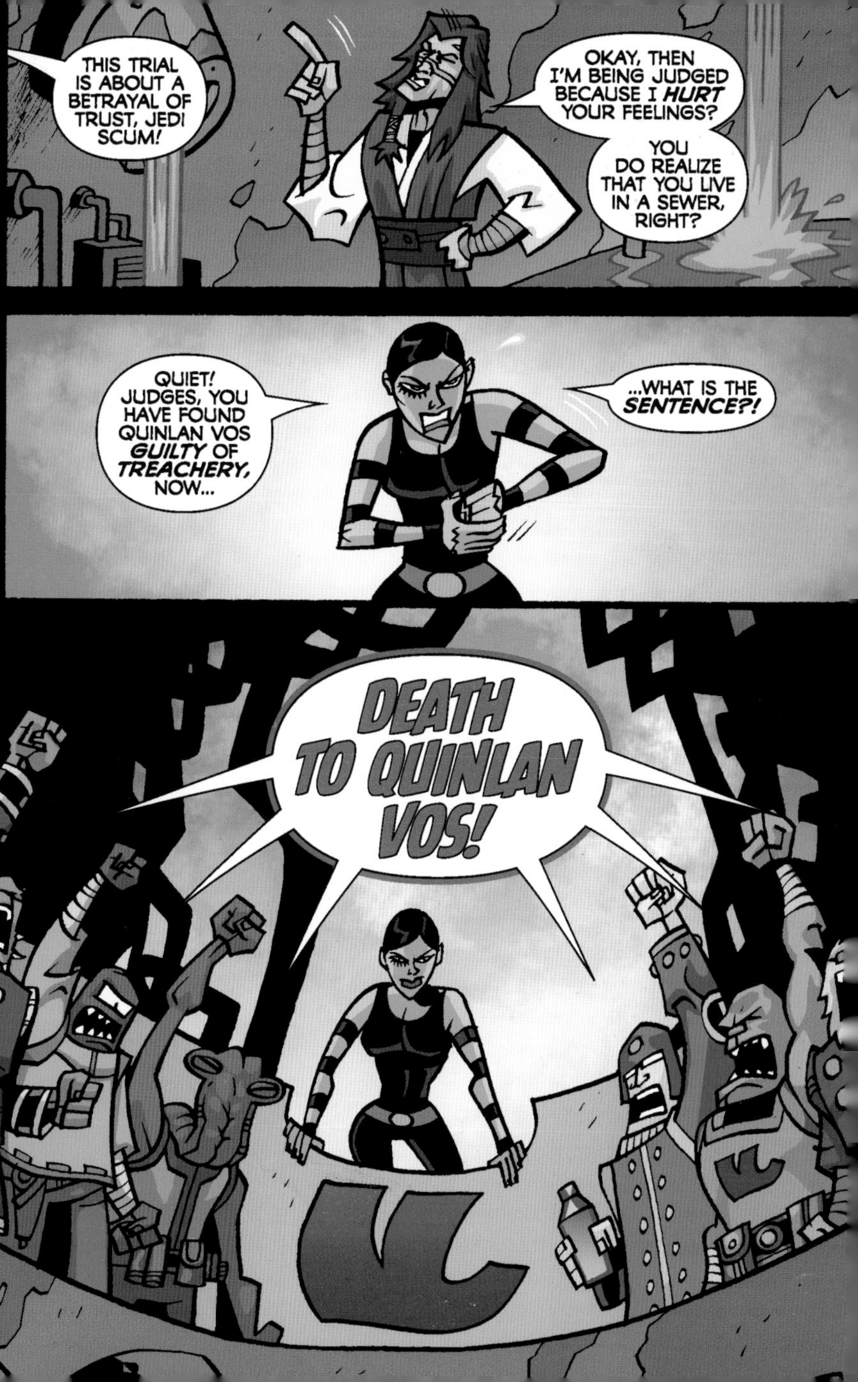
THIS TRIAL IS ABOUT A BETRAYAL OF TRUST, JEDI SCUM!
OKAY, THEN I'M BEING JUDGED BECAUSE I *HURT* YOUR FEELINGS?
YOU DO REALIZE THAT YOU LIVE IN A SEWER, RIGHT?
QUIET! JUDGES, YOU HAVE FOUND QUINLAN VOS *GUILTY* OF *TREACHERY,* NOW...
...WHAT IS THE *SENTENCE?!*
DEATH TO QUINLAN VOS!

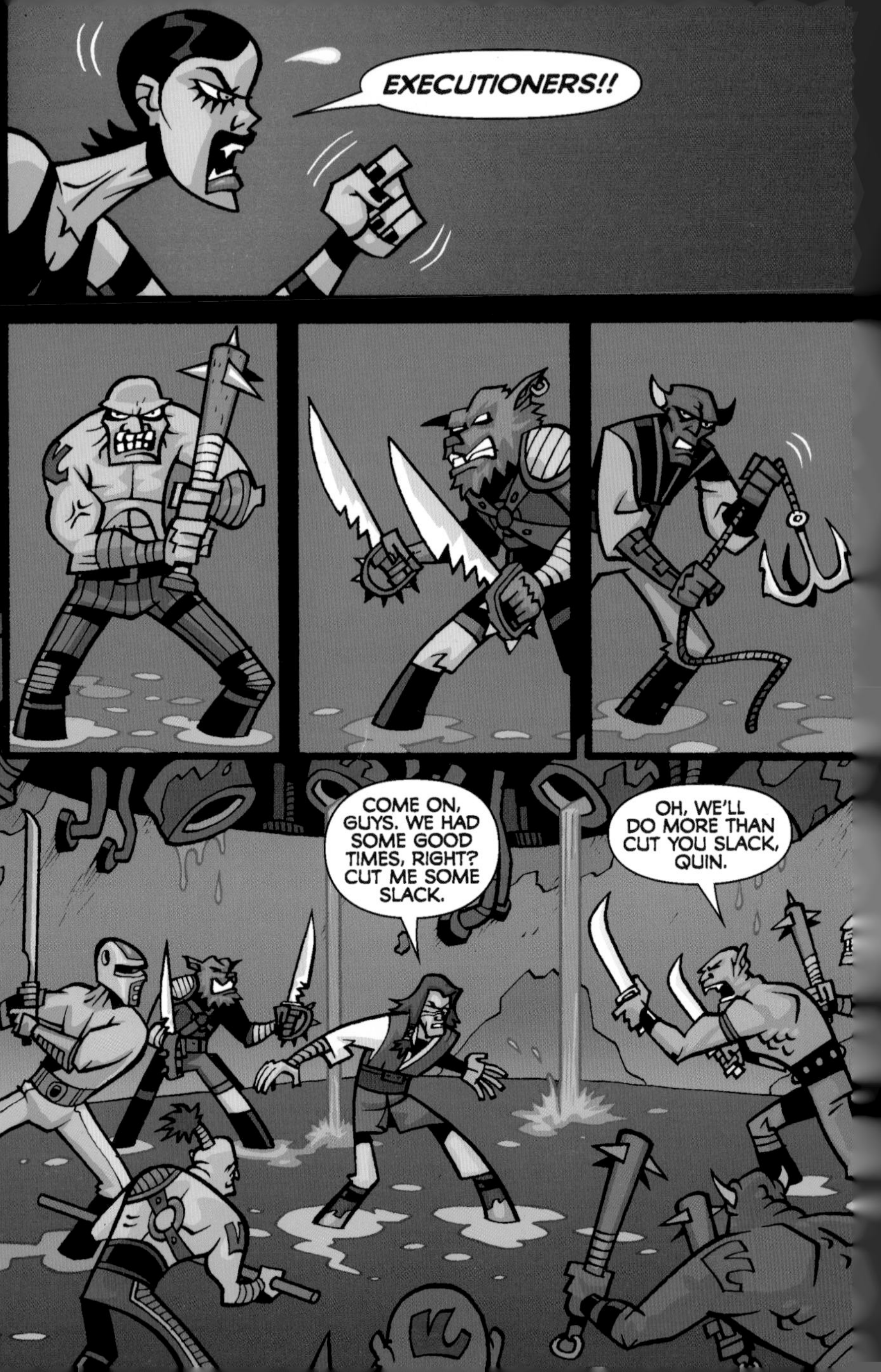
EXECUTIONERS!!
COME ON, GUYS. WE HAD SOME GOOD TIMES, RIGHT? CUT ME SOME SLACK.
OH, WE'LL DO MORE THAN CUT YOU SLACK, QUIN.

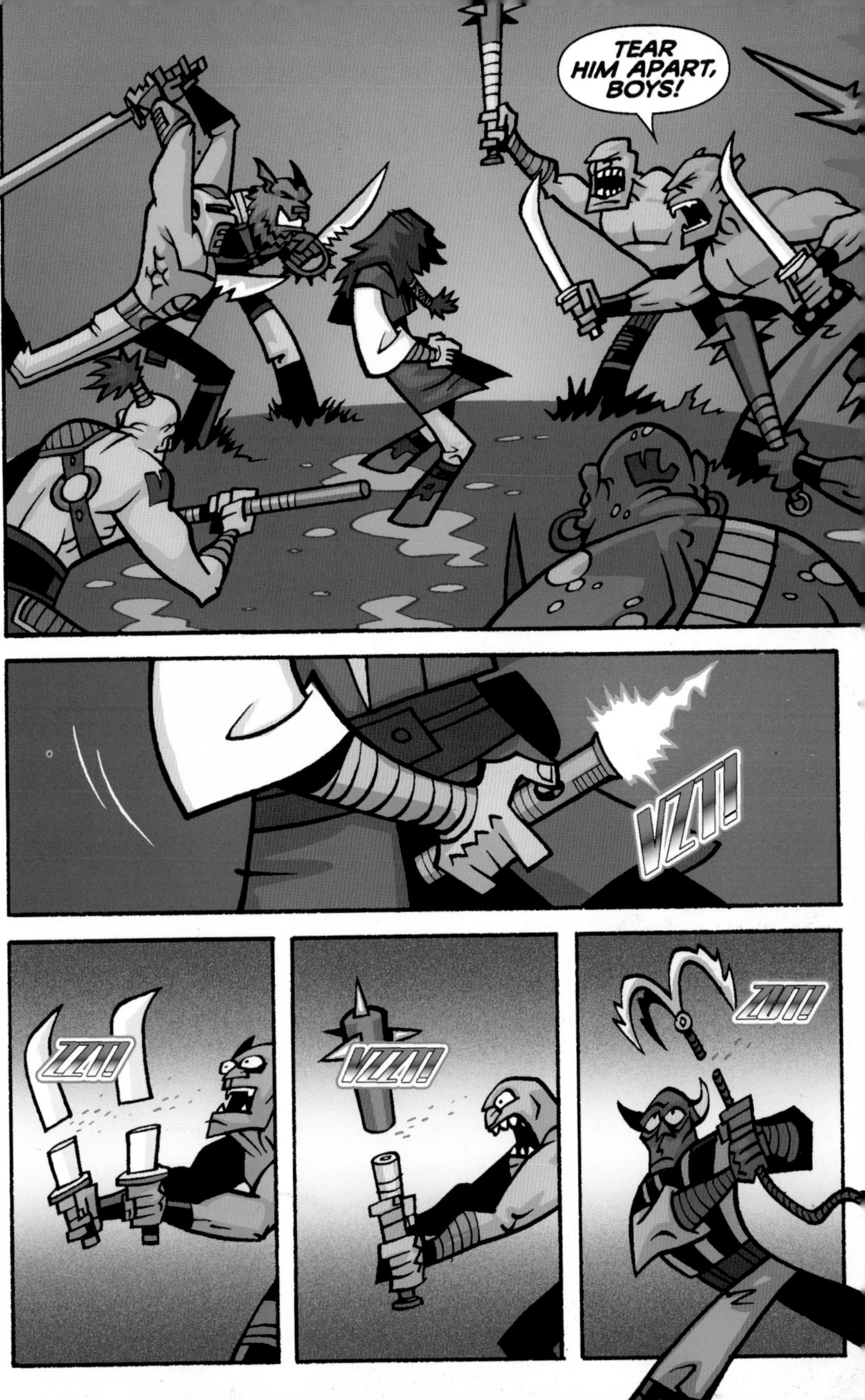
TEAR HIM APART, BOYS!
VZT!
ZZT!
VZZT!
ZUT!

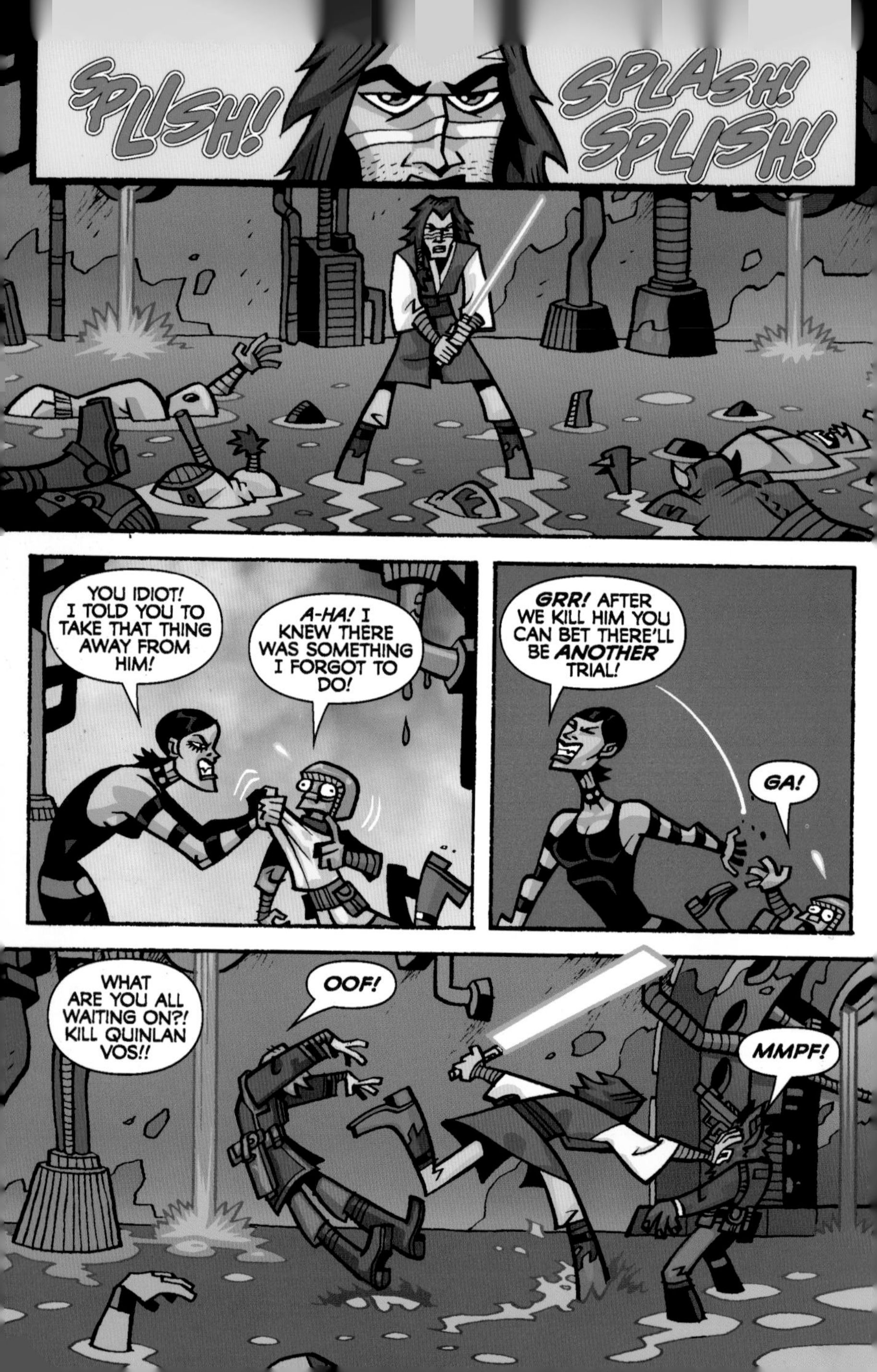
SPLISH!
SPLASH! SPLISH!
YOU IDIOT! I TOLD YOU TO TAKE THAT THING AWAY FROM HIM!
A-HA! I KNEW THERE WAS SOMETHING I FORGOT TO DO!
GRR! AFTER WE KILL HIM YOU CAN BET THERE'LL BE ANOTHER TRIAL!
GA!
WHAT ARE YOU ALL WAITING ON?! KILL QUINLAN VOS!!
OOF!
MMPF!

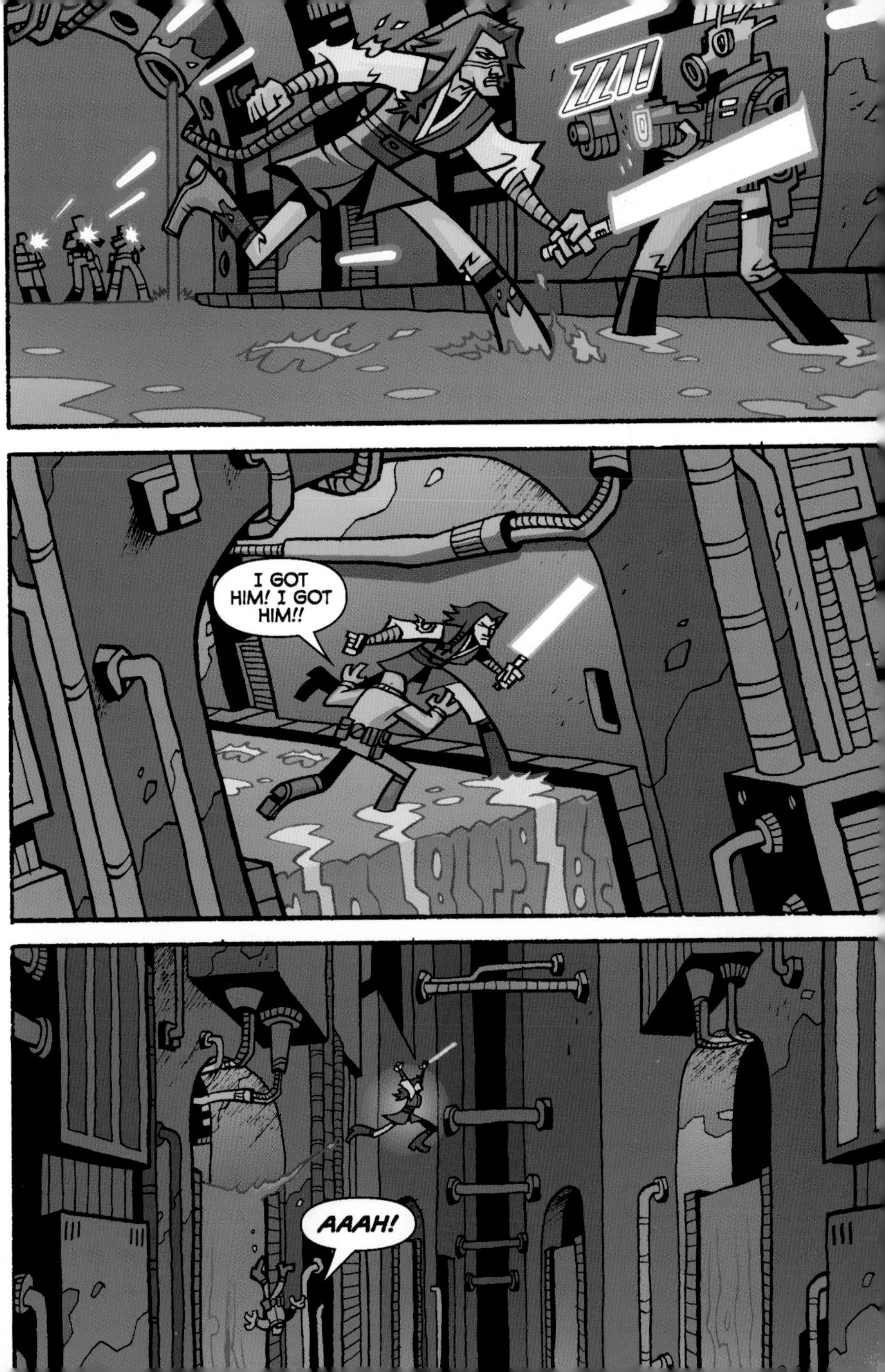

ZZAT!
I GOT HIM! I GOT HIM!!
AAAH!

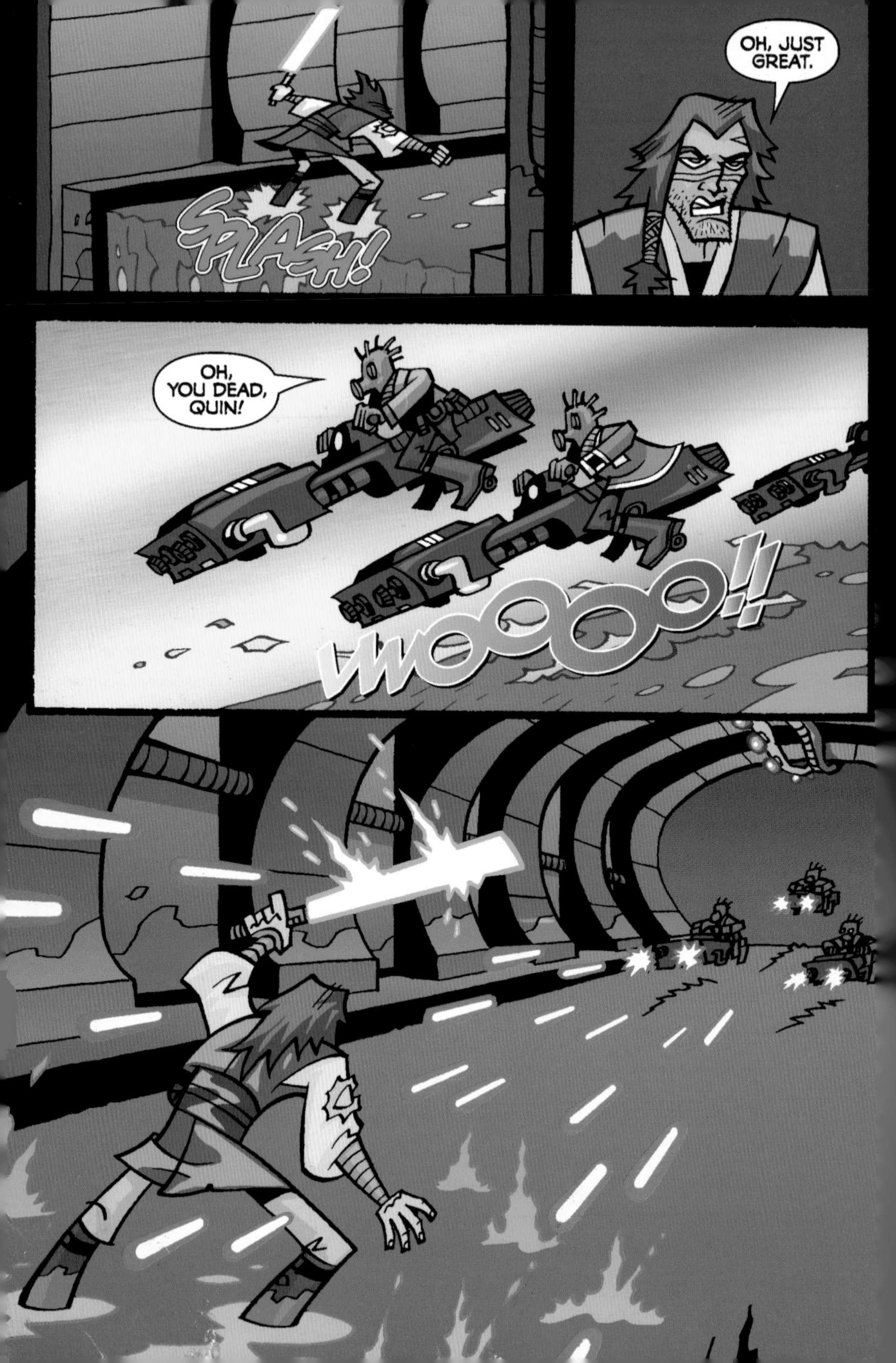
SPLASH!
OH, JUST GREAT.
OH, YOU DEAD, QUIN!
VWOOOOO!!

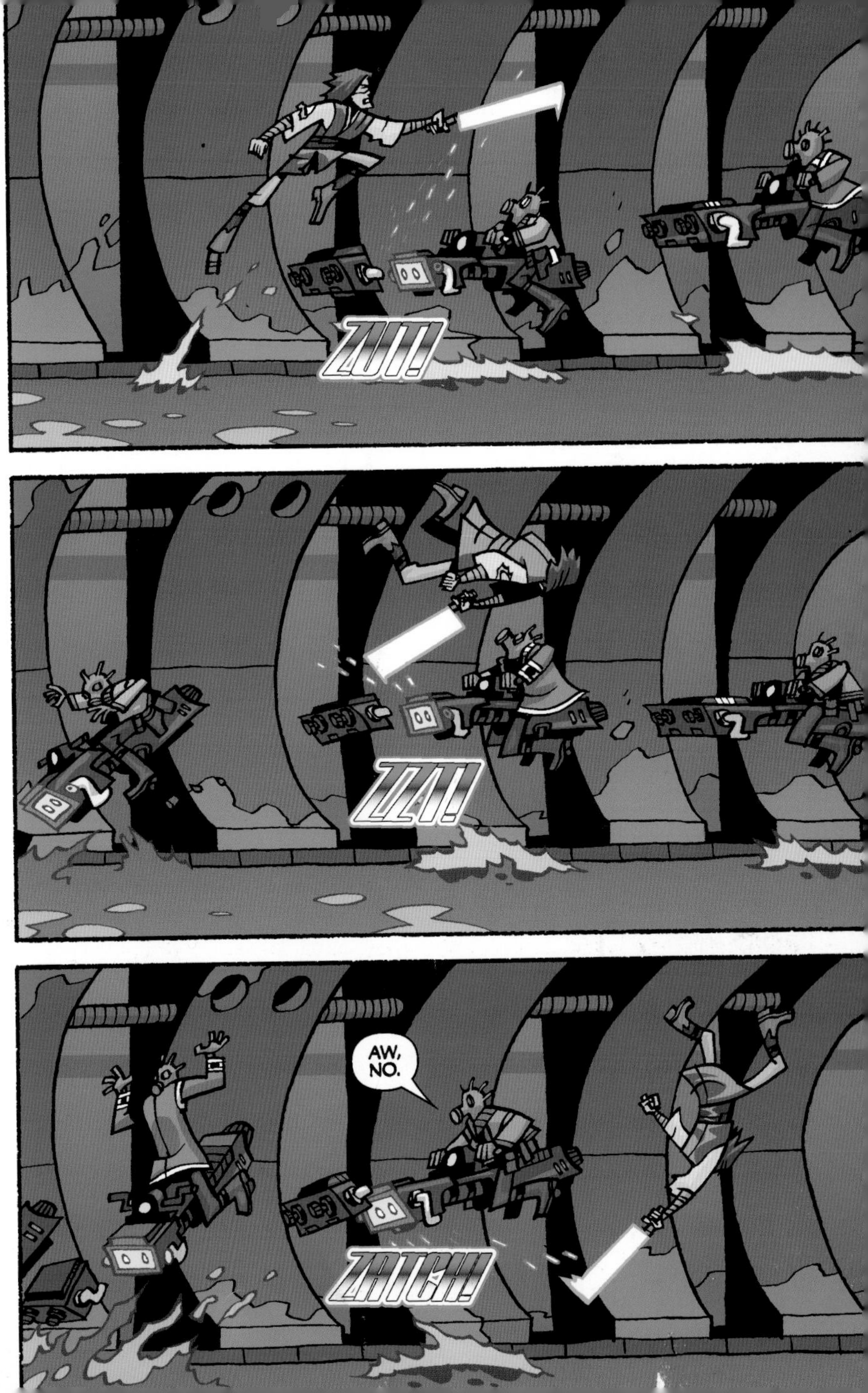
ZUT!
ZZAT!
AW, NO.
ZATCH!

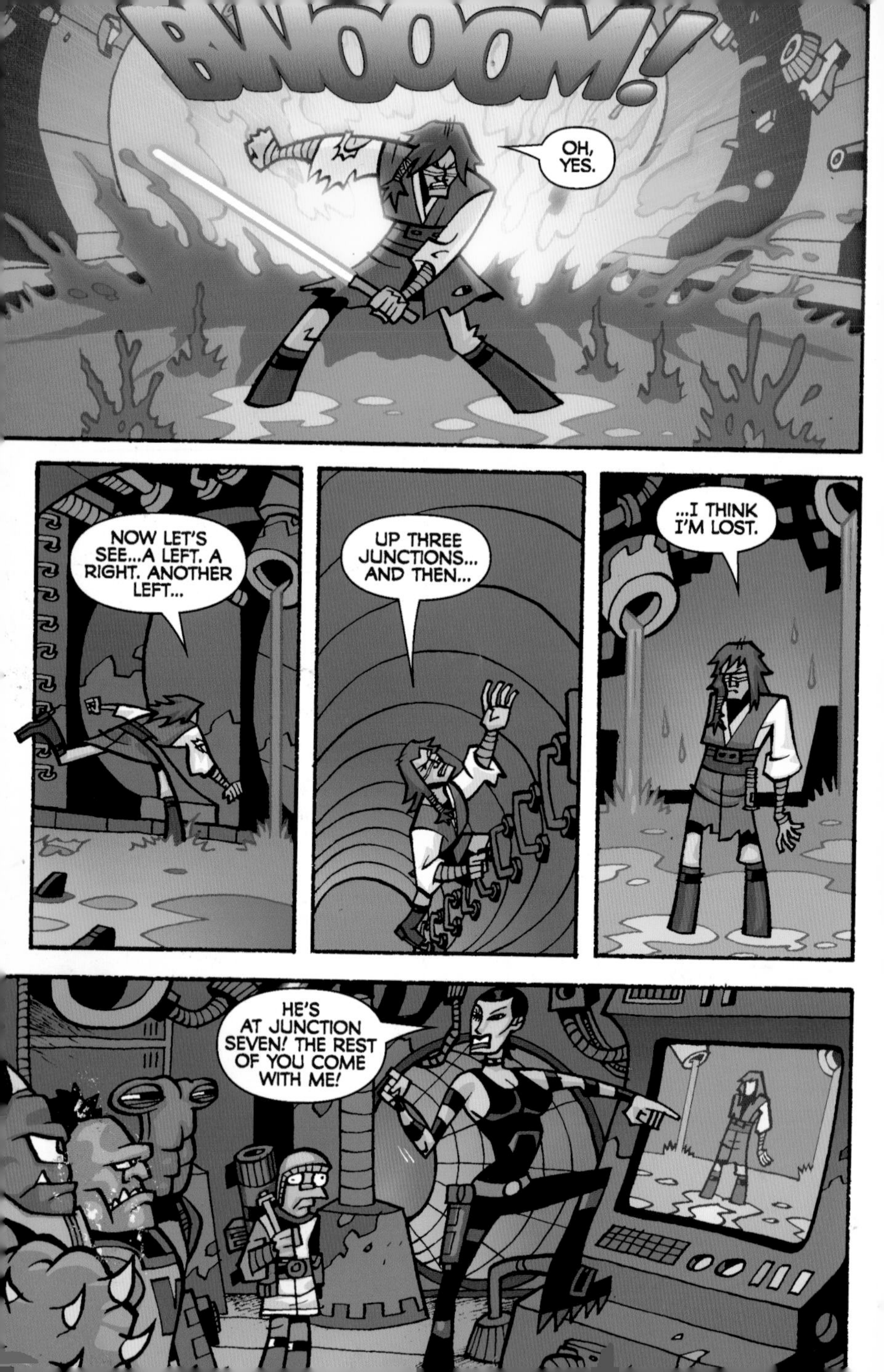
BWOOOM!
OH, YES.
NOW LET'S SEE...A LEFT. A RIGHT. ANOTHER LEFT...
UP THREE JUNCTIONS... AND THEN...
...I THINK I'M LOST.
HE'S AT JUNCTION SEVEN! THE REST OF YOU COME WITH ME!

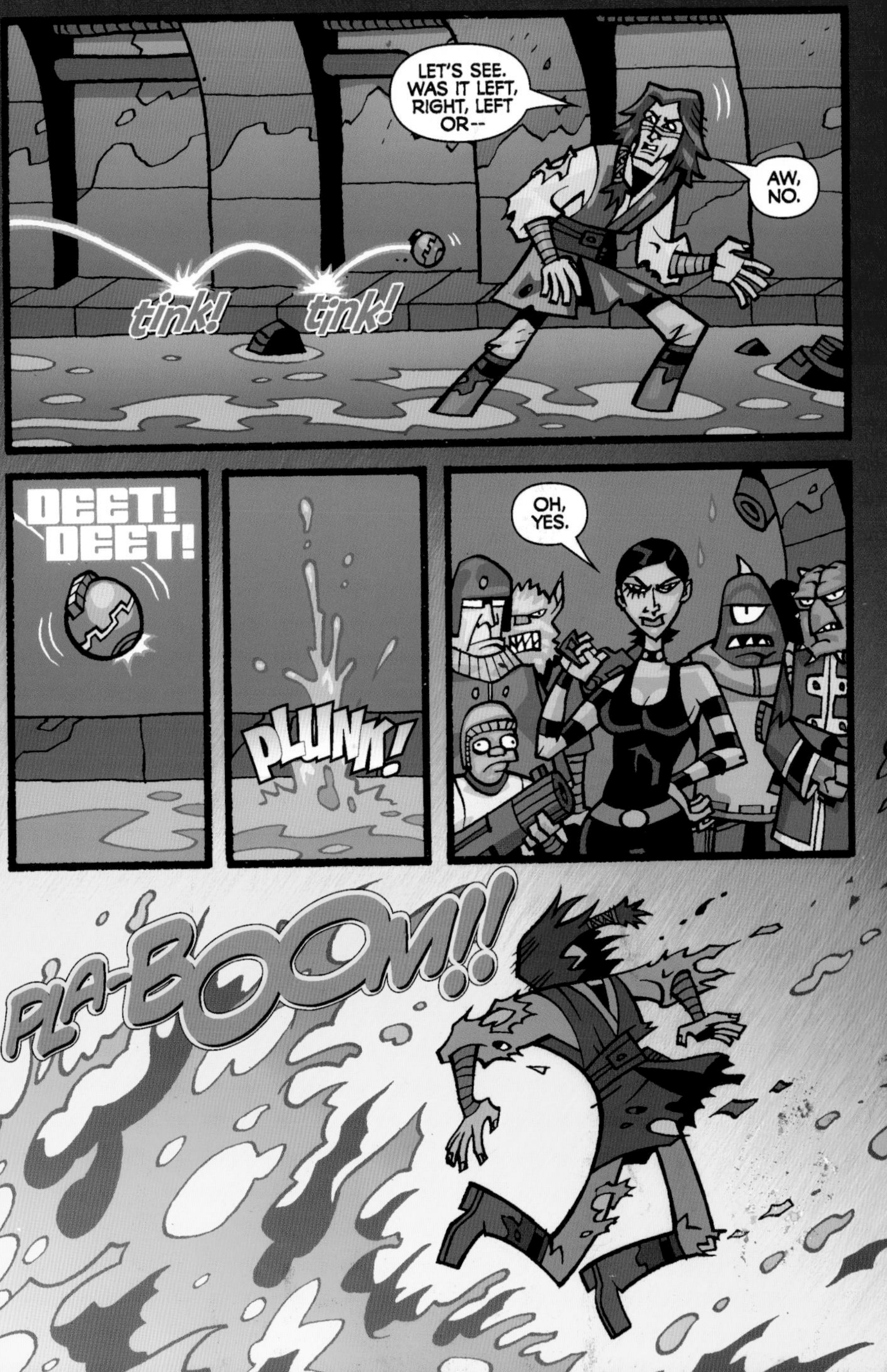
LET'S SEE. WAS IT LEFT, RIGHT, LEFT OR--
AW, NO.
tink!
tink!
DEET! DEET!
PLUNK!
OH, YES.
PLA-BOOM!!

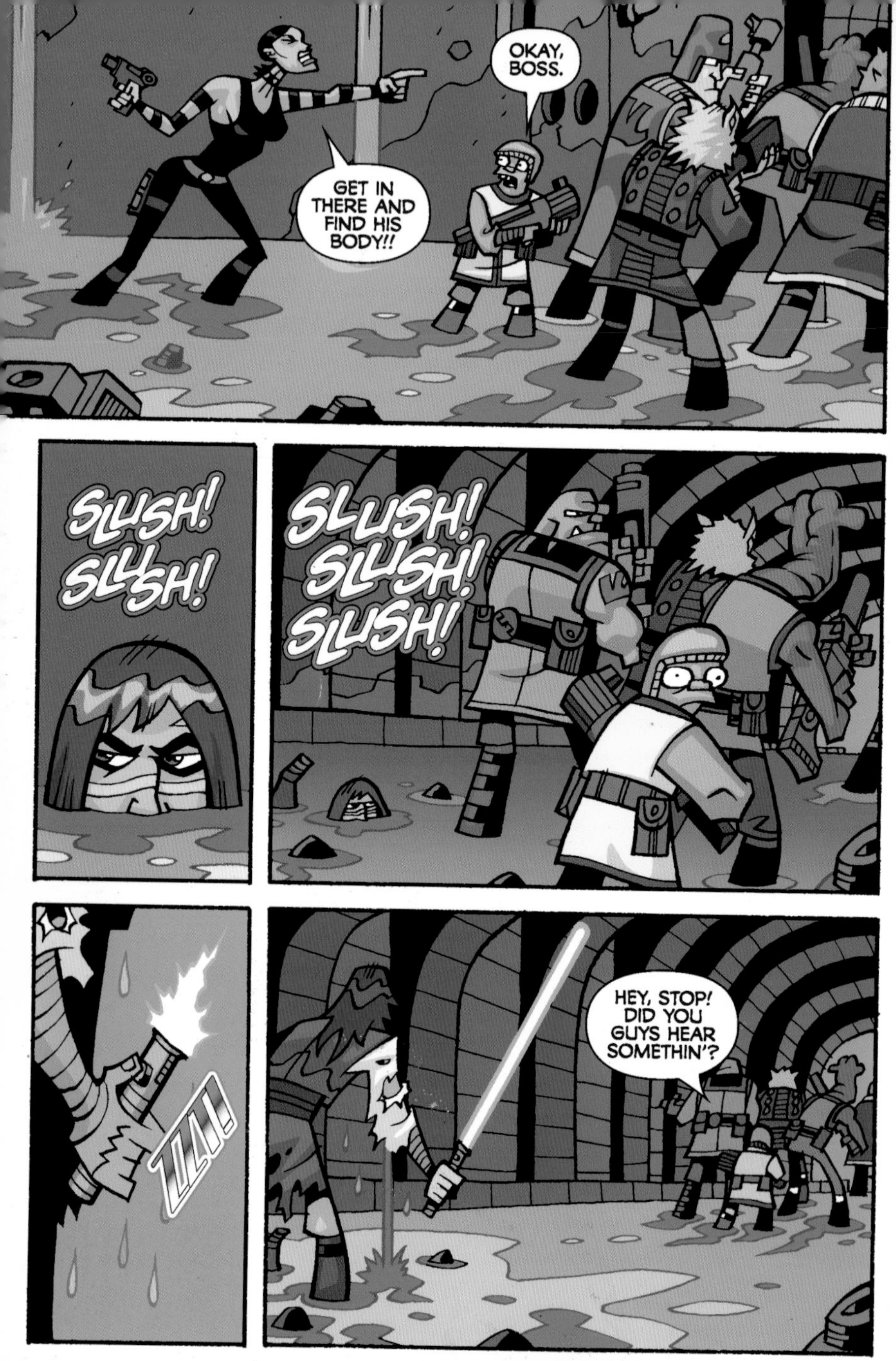
GET IN THERE AND FIND HIS BODY!!
OKAY, BOSS.
SLUSH! SLUSH!
SLUSH! SLUSH! SLUSH!
HEY, STOP! DID YOU GUYS HEAR SOMETHIN'?

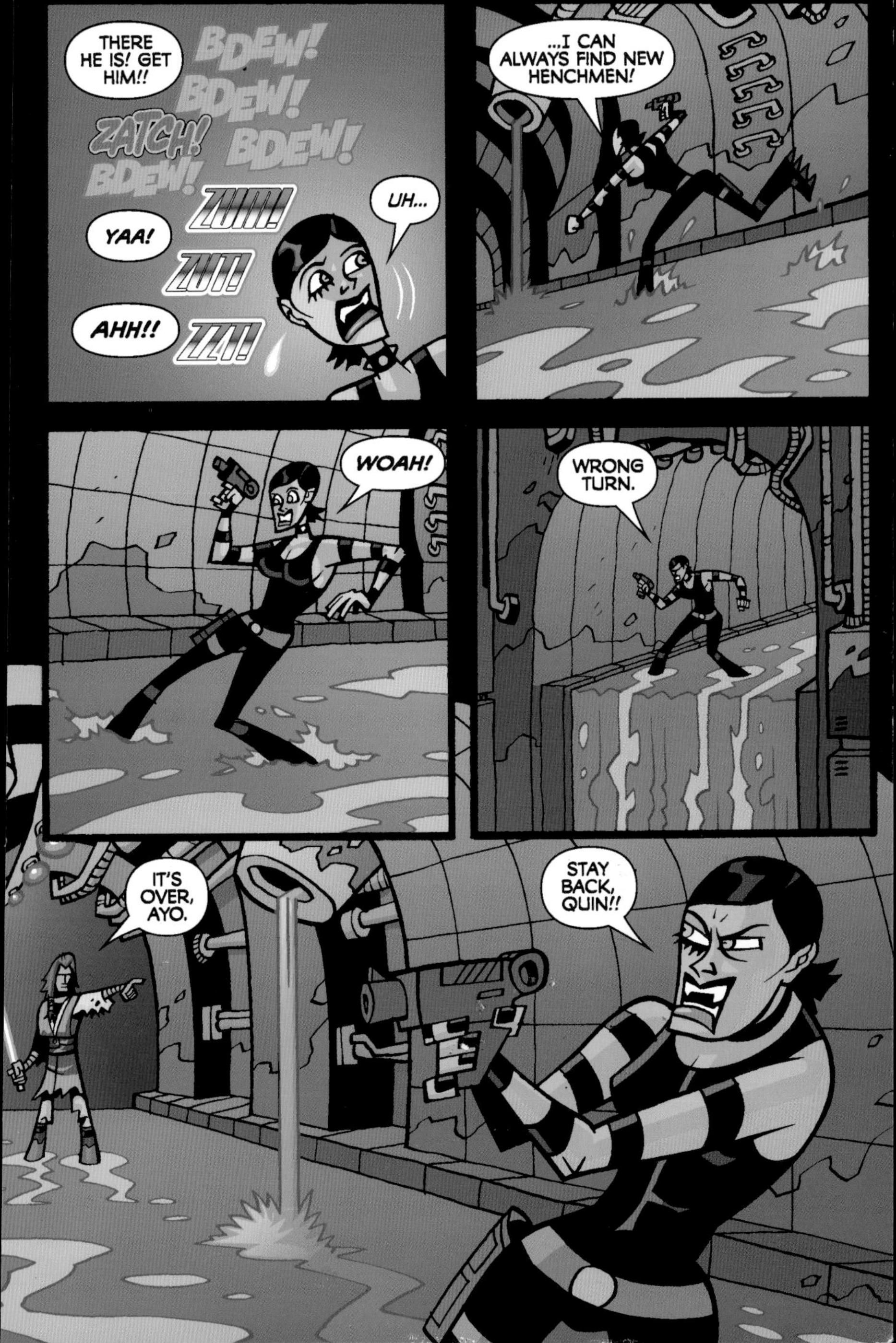
THERE HE IS! GET HIM!!
BDEW!
BDEW!
ZATCH!
BDEW!
BDEW!
ZUM!
YAA!
ZUT!
AHH!!
ZZT!
UH...
...I CAN ALWAYS FIND NEW HENCHMEN!
WOAH!
WRONG TURN.
IT'S OVER, AYO.
STAY BACK, QUIN!!

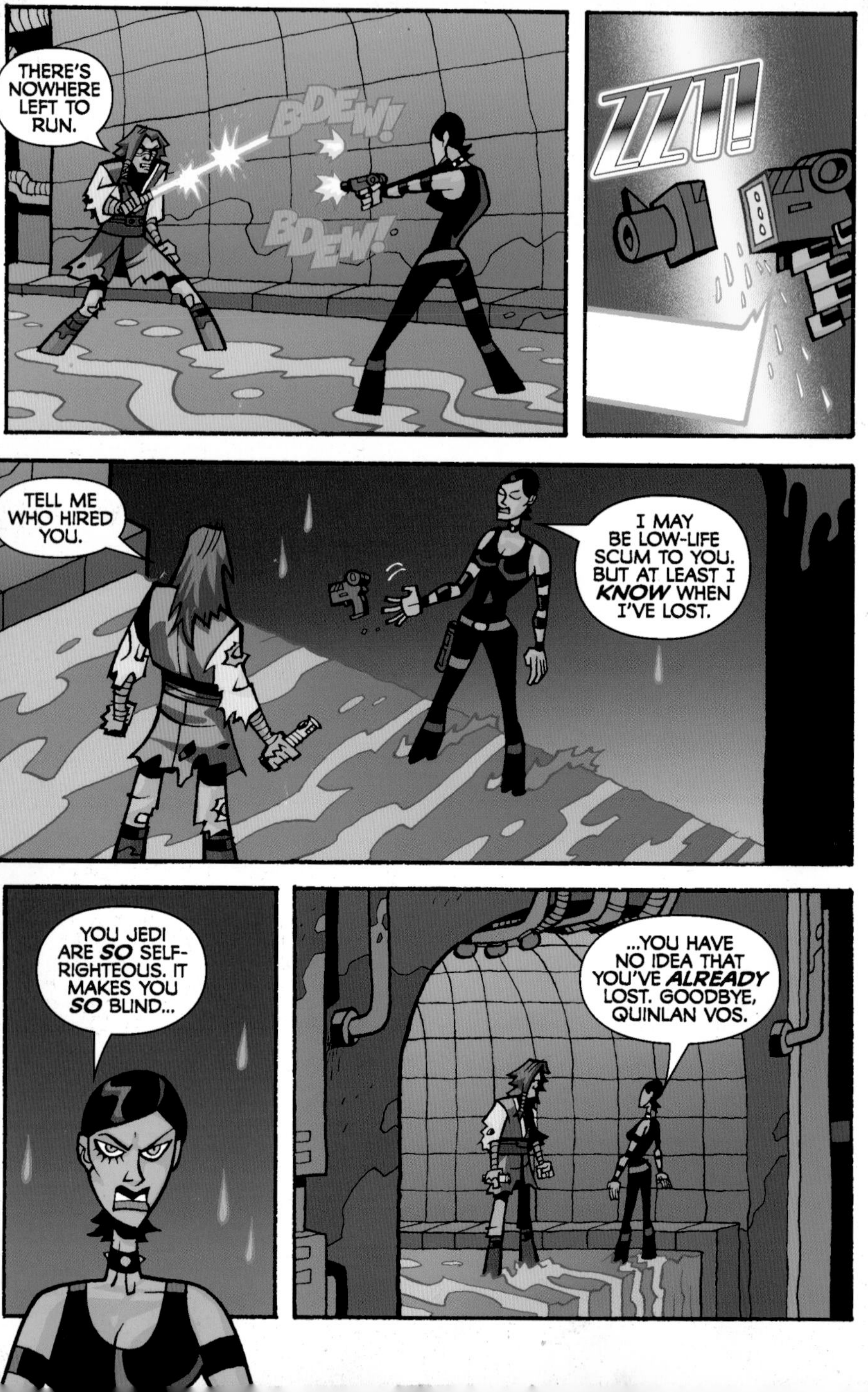
THERE'S NOWHERE LEFT TO RUN.
BDEW!
BDEW!
ZZZT!
TELL ME WHO HIRED YOU.
I MAY BE LOW-LIFE SCUM TO YOU. BUT AT LEAST I KNOW WHEN I'VE LOST.
YOU JEDI ARE SO SELF-RIGHTEOUS. IT MAKES YOU SO BLIND...
...YOU HAVE NO IDEA THAT YOU'VE ALREADY LOST. GOODBYE, QUINLAN VOS.

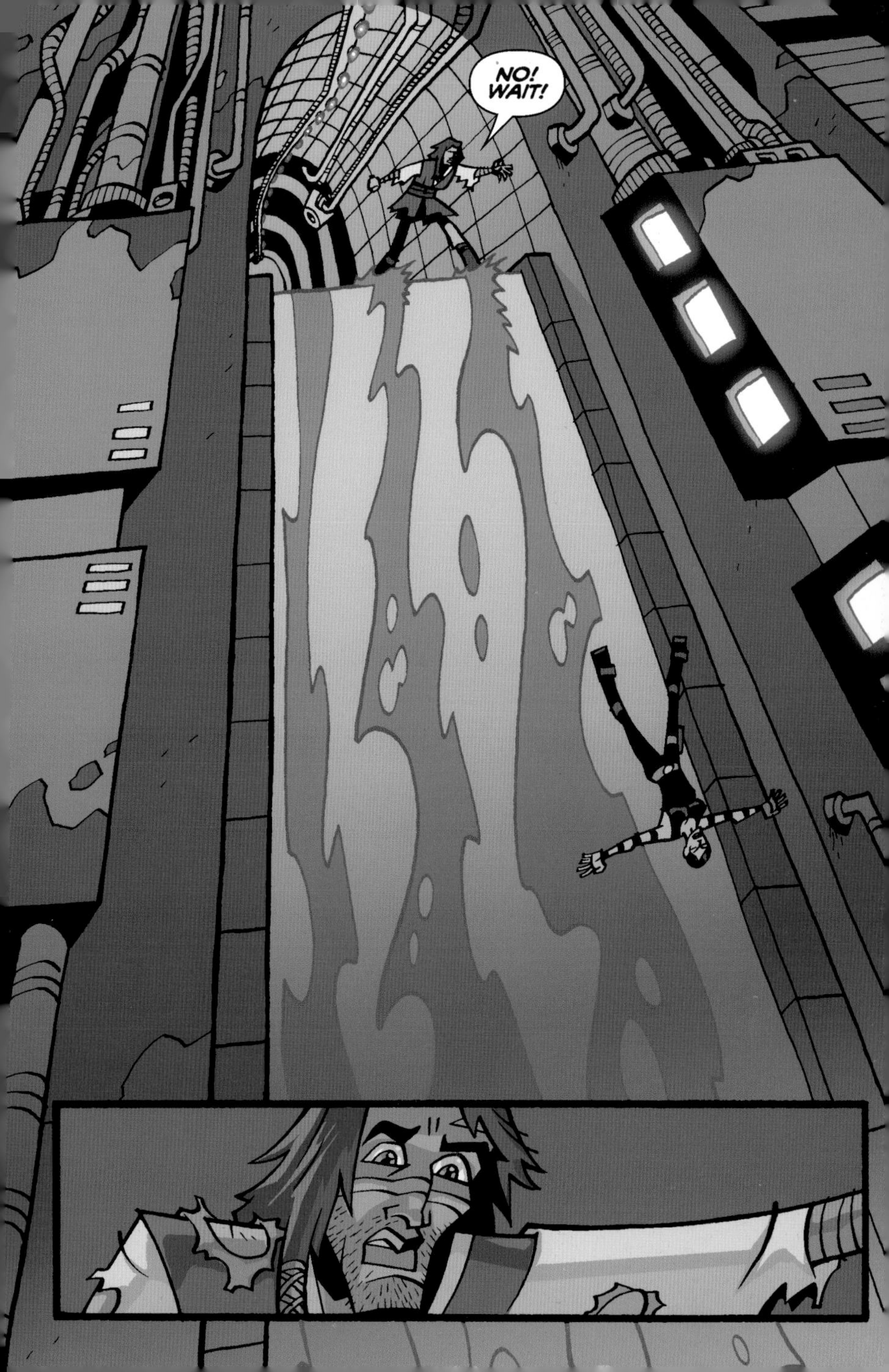
NO! WAIT!

...

WHAT EVIL COULD COMMAND SUCH LOYALTY THAT AYO WOULD TAKE HER OWN LIFE TO PROTECT IT?

LOYALTY...? PERHAPS.

BUT *FEAR...*

"...*FEAR* CAN MAKE ONE WHO LIVES BELOW A SLAVE TO THE ONE LIVING IN THE HIGHEST TOWER."

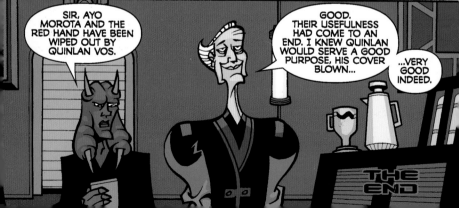

SIR, AYO MOROTA AND THE RED HAND HAVE BEEN WIPED OUT BY QUINLAN VOS.

GOOD. THEIR USEFULNESS HAD COME TO AN END. I KNEW QUINLAN WOULD SERVE A GOOD PURPOSE, HIS COVER BLOWN...

...VERY GOOD INDEED.

THE END

A CLONE WARS ADVENTURE

MACE WINDU in NO WAY OUT

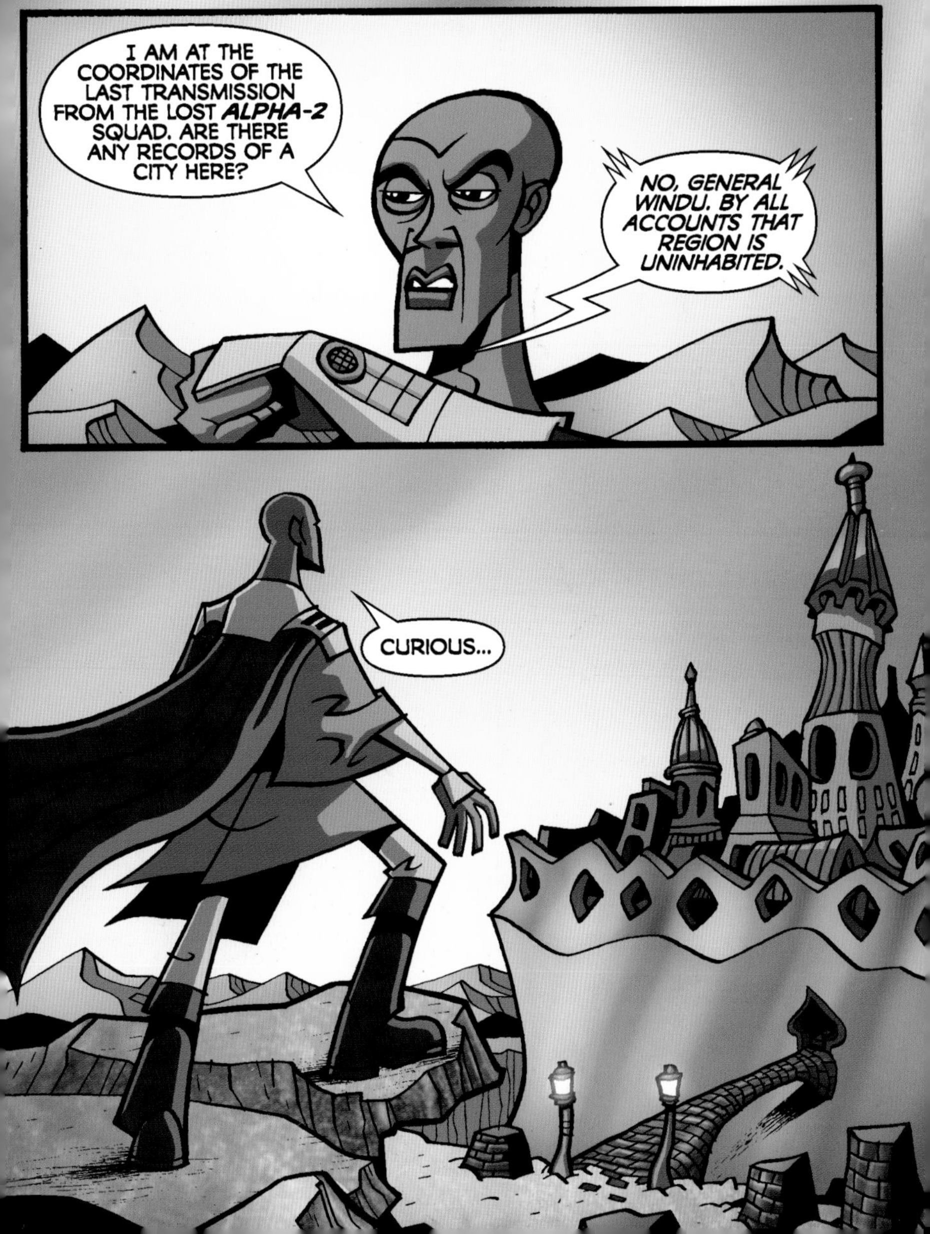
I AM AT THE COORDINATES OF THE LAST TRANSMISSION FROM THE LOST *ALPHA-2* SQUAD. ARE THERE ANY RECORDS OF A CITY HERE?
NO, GENERAL WINDU. BY ALL ACCOUNTS THAT REGION IS UNINHABITED.
CURIOUS...

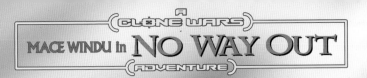

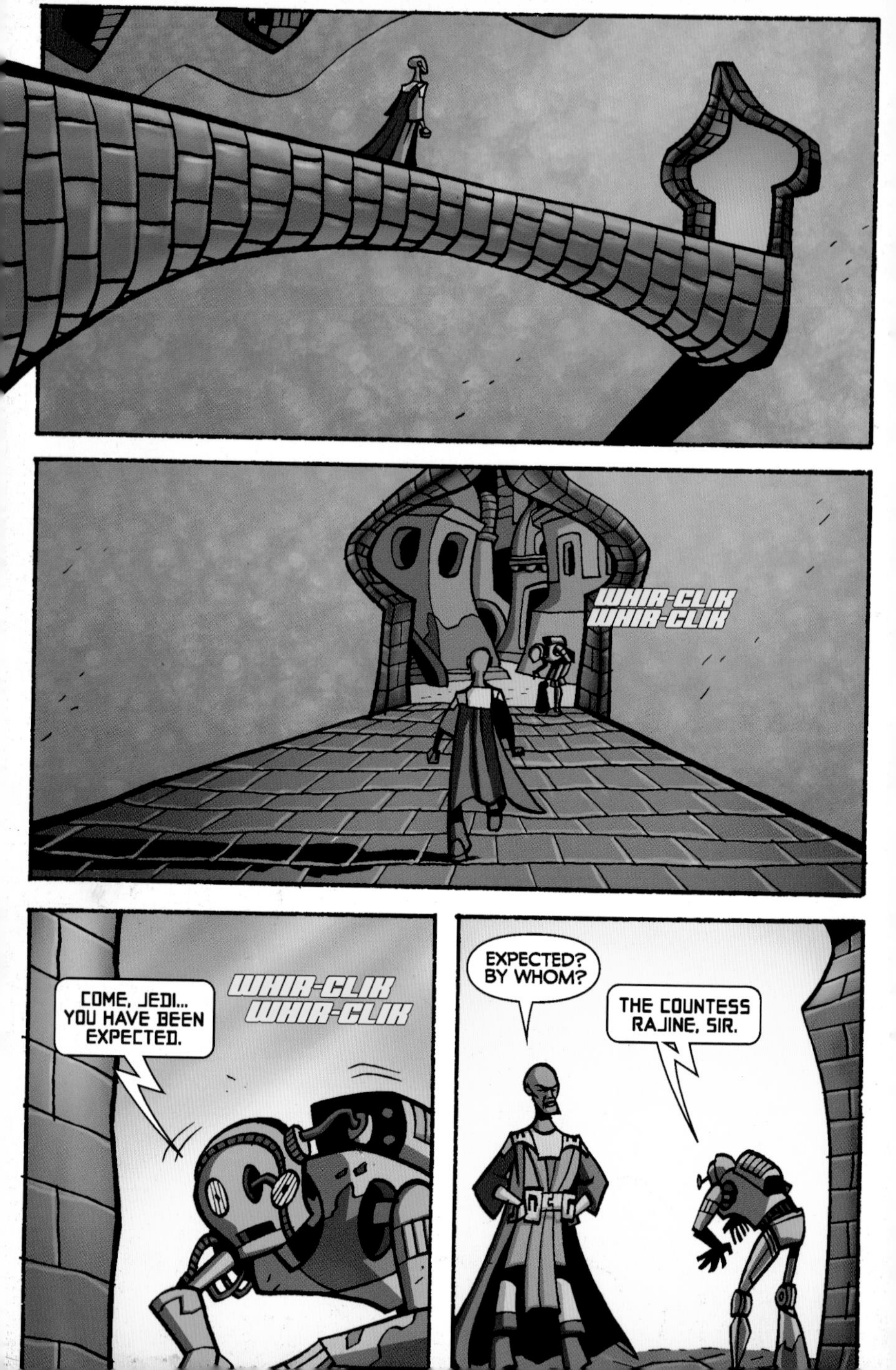
WHIR-CLIK
WHIR-CLIK
COME, JEDI... YOU HAVE BEEN EXPECTED.
WHIR-CLIK
WHIR-CLIK
EXPECTED? BY WHOM?
THE COUNTESS RAJINE, SIR.

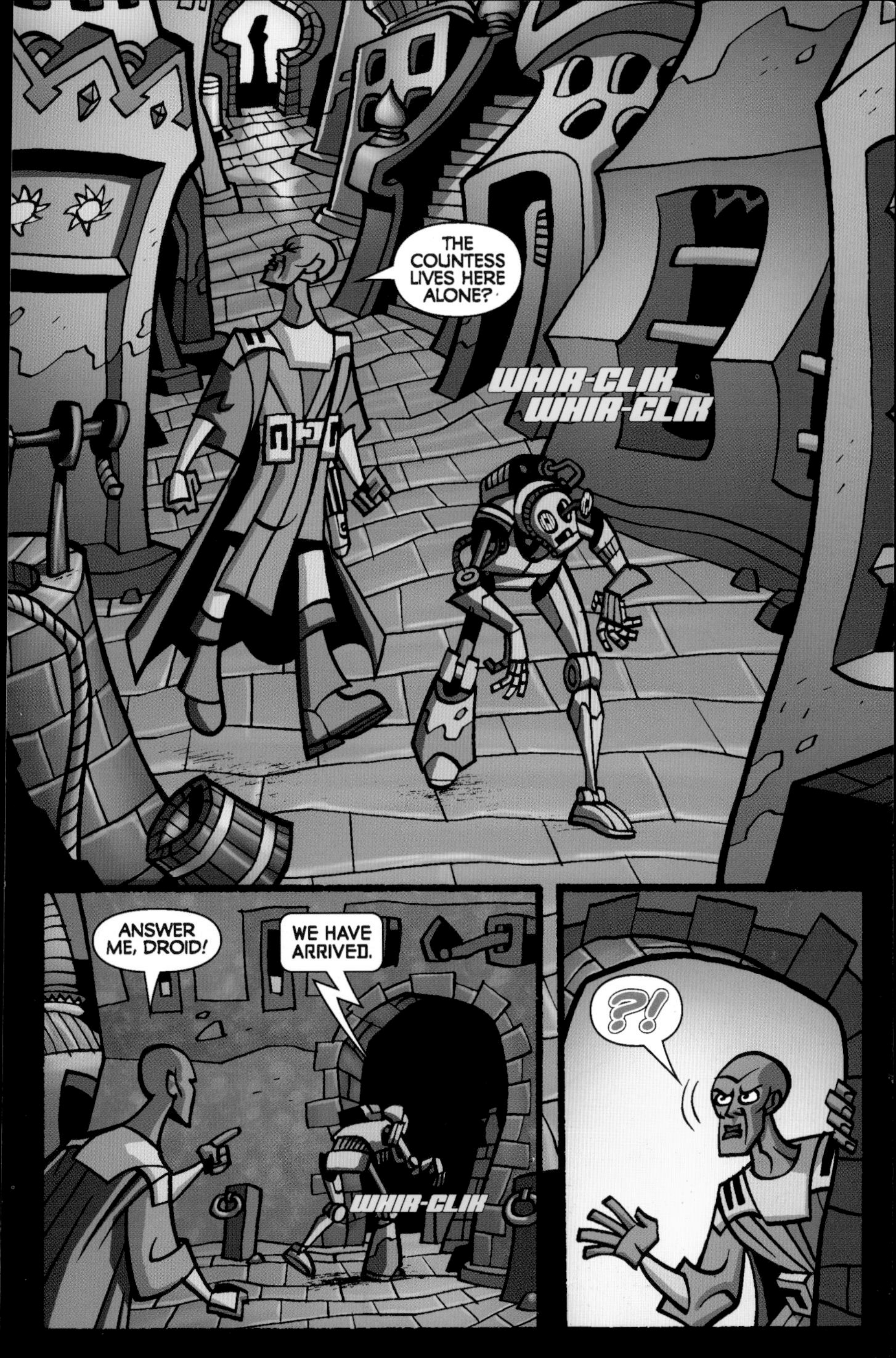
THE COUNTESS LIVES HERE ALONE?
WHIR-CLIK
WHIR-CLIK
ANSWER ME, DROID!
WE HAVE ARRIVED.
WHIR-CLIK
?!

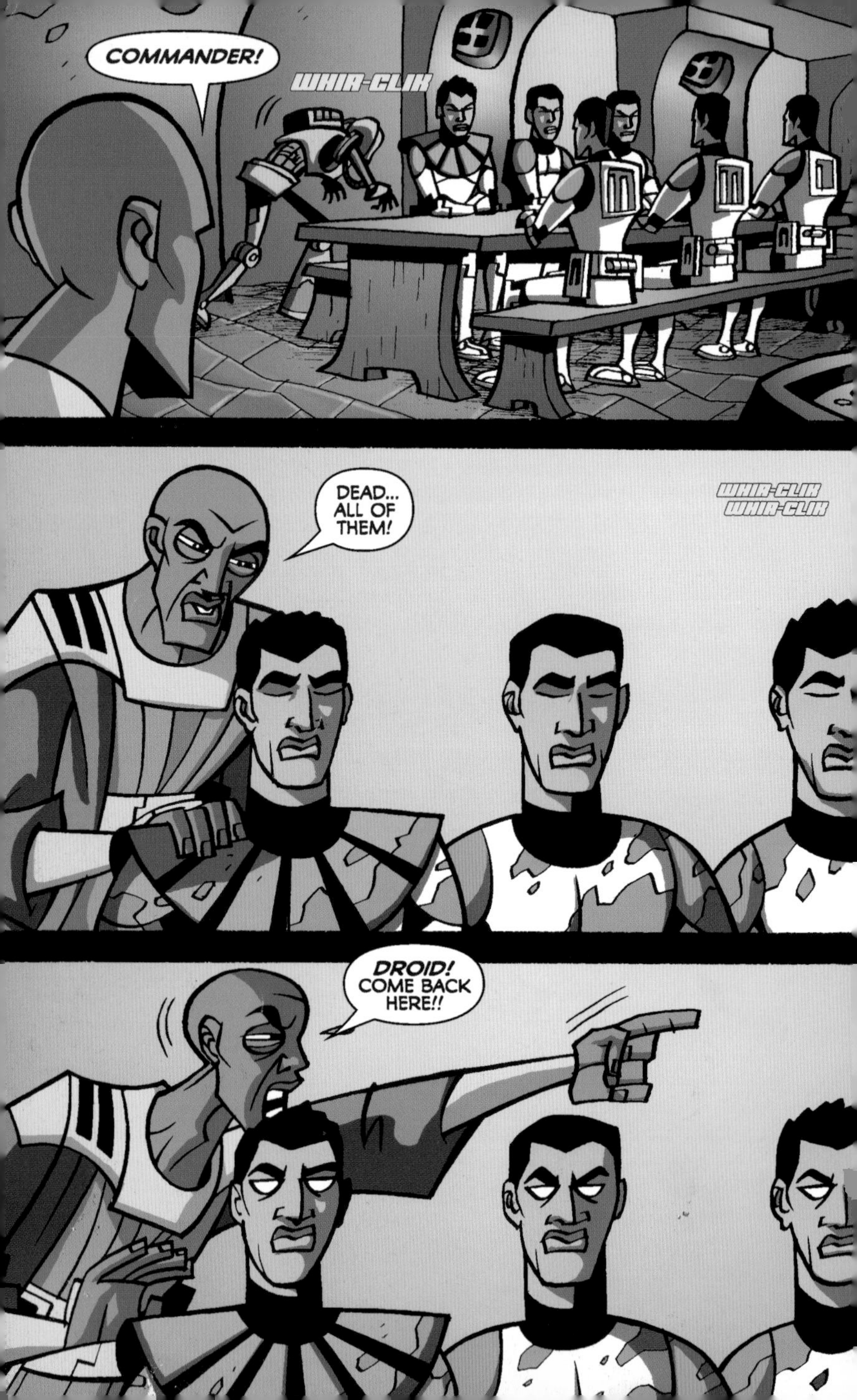
COMMANDER!
WHIR-CLIK
DEAD... ALL OF THEM!
WHIR-CLIK
WHIR-CLIK
DROID! COME BACK HERE!!

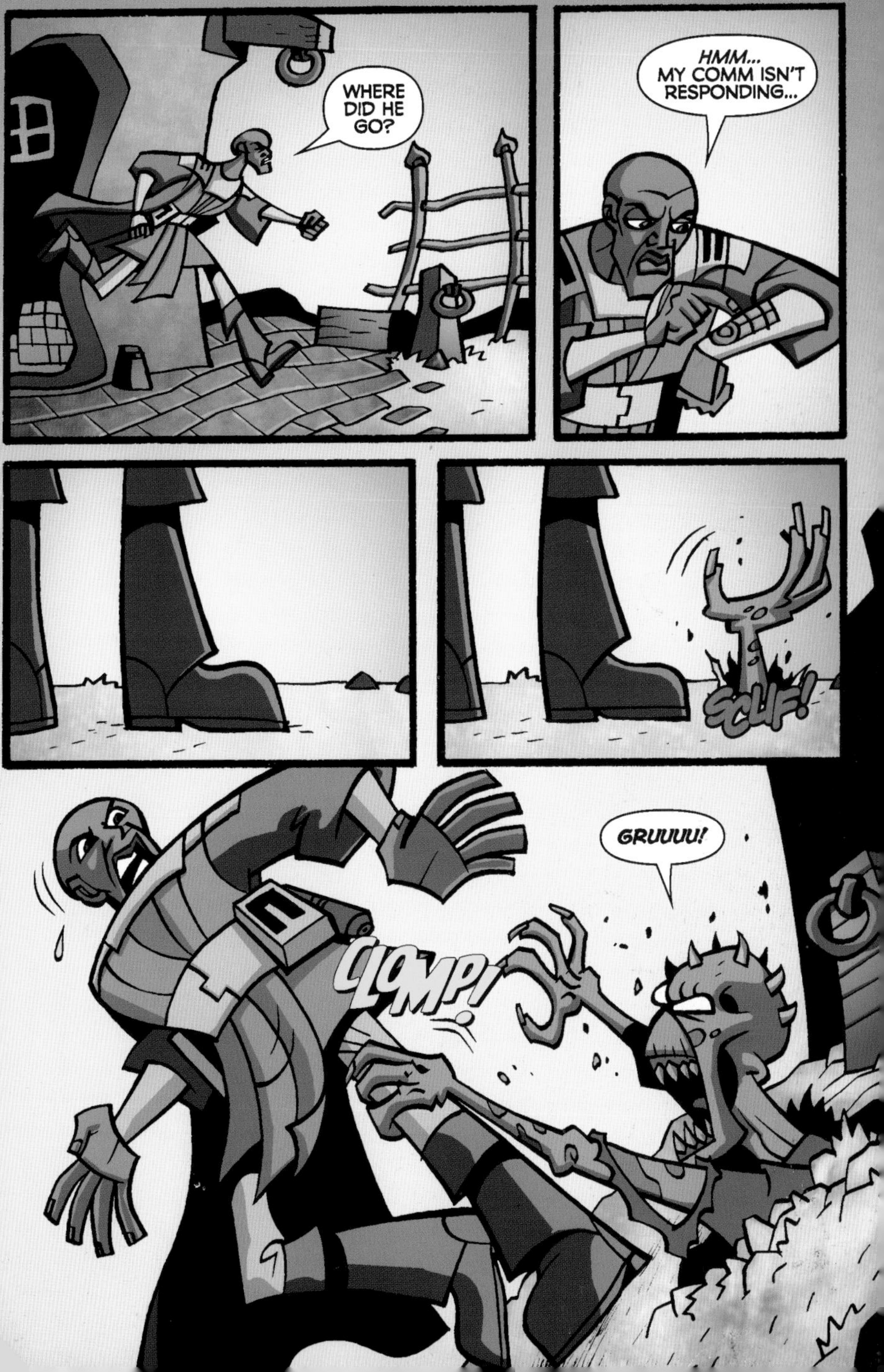
WHERE DID HE GO?
HMM... MY COMM ISN'T RESPONDING...
SCUF!
GRUUUU!
CLOMP!

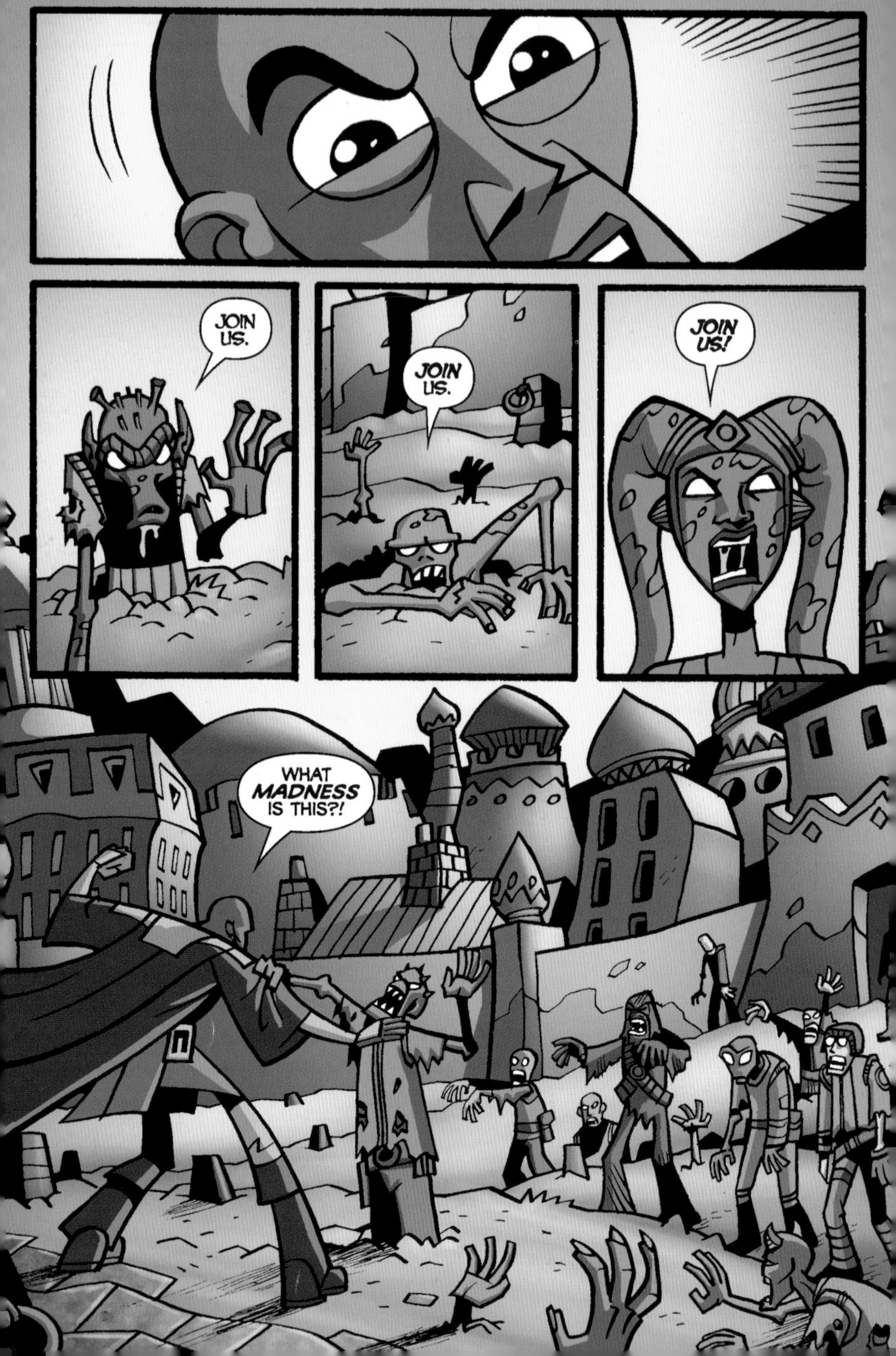
JOIN US.
JOIN US.
JOIN US!
WHAT MADNESS IS THIS?!

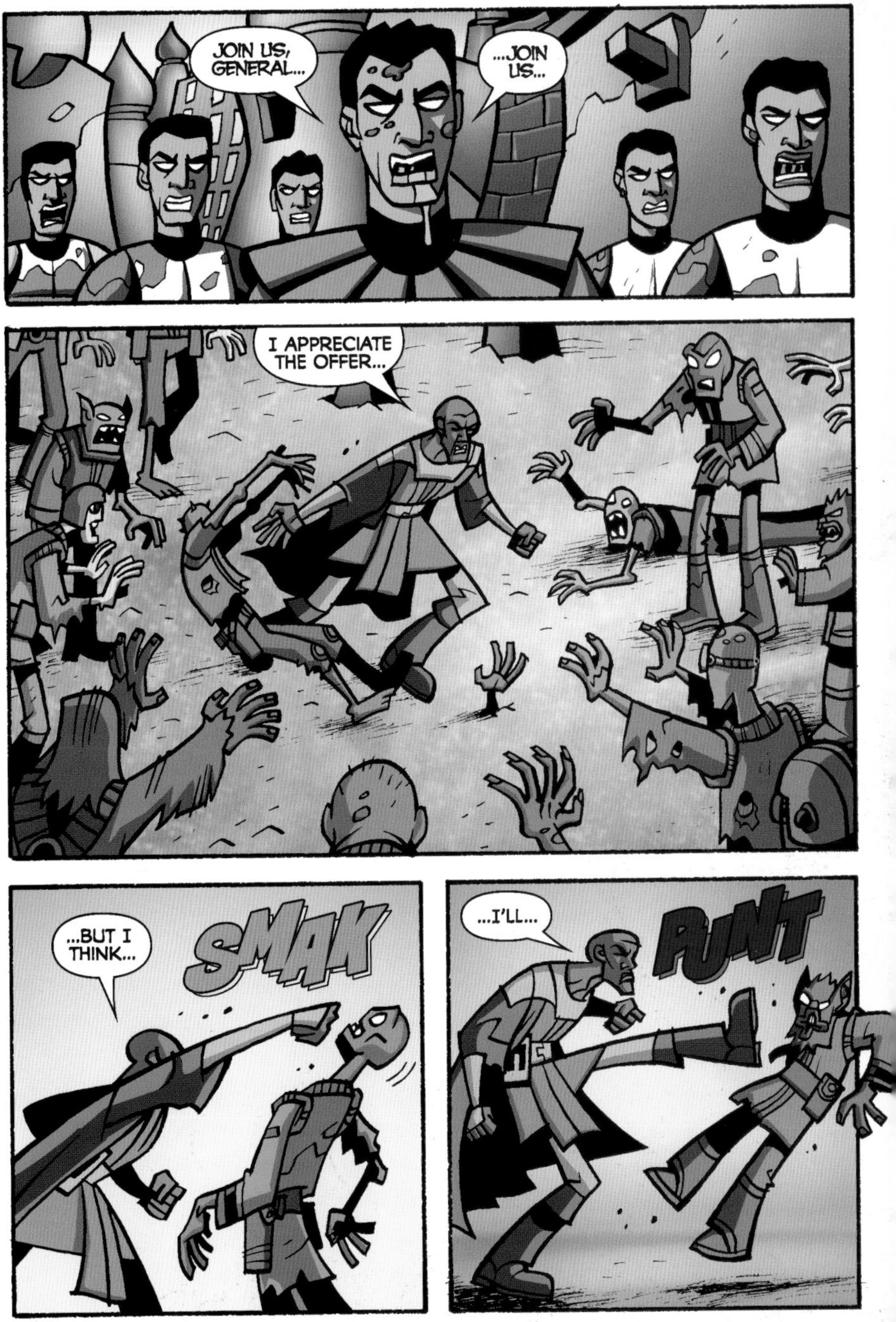
JOIN US, GENERAL...
...JOIN US...
I APPRECIATE THE OFFER...
...BUT I THINK...
SMAK
...I'LL...
PUNT

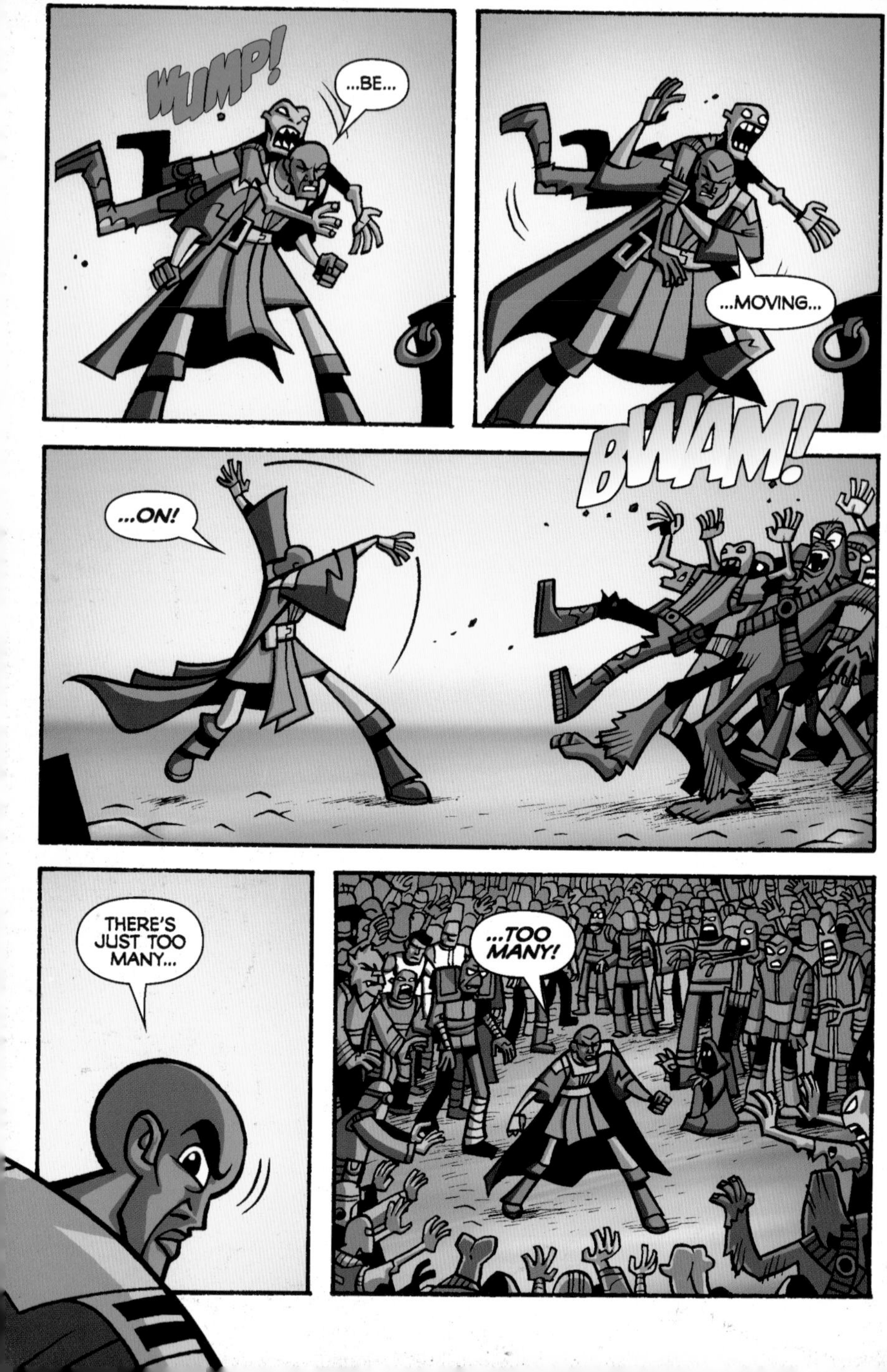
WUMP!
...BE...
...MOVING...
BWAM!
...ON!
THERE'S JUST TOO MANY...
...TOO MANY!

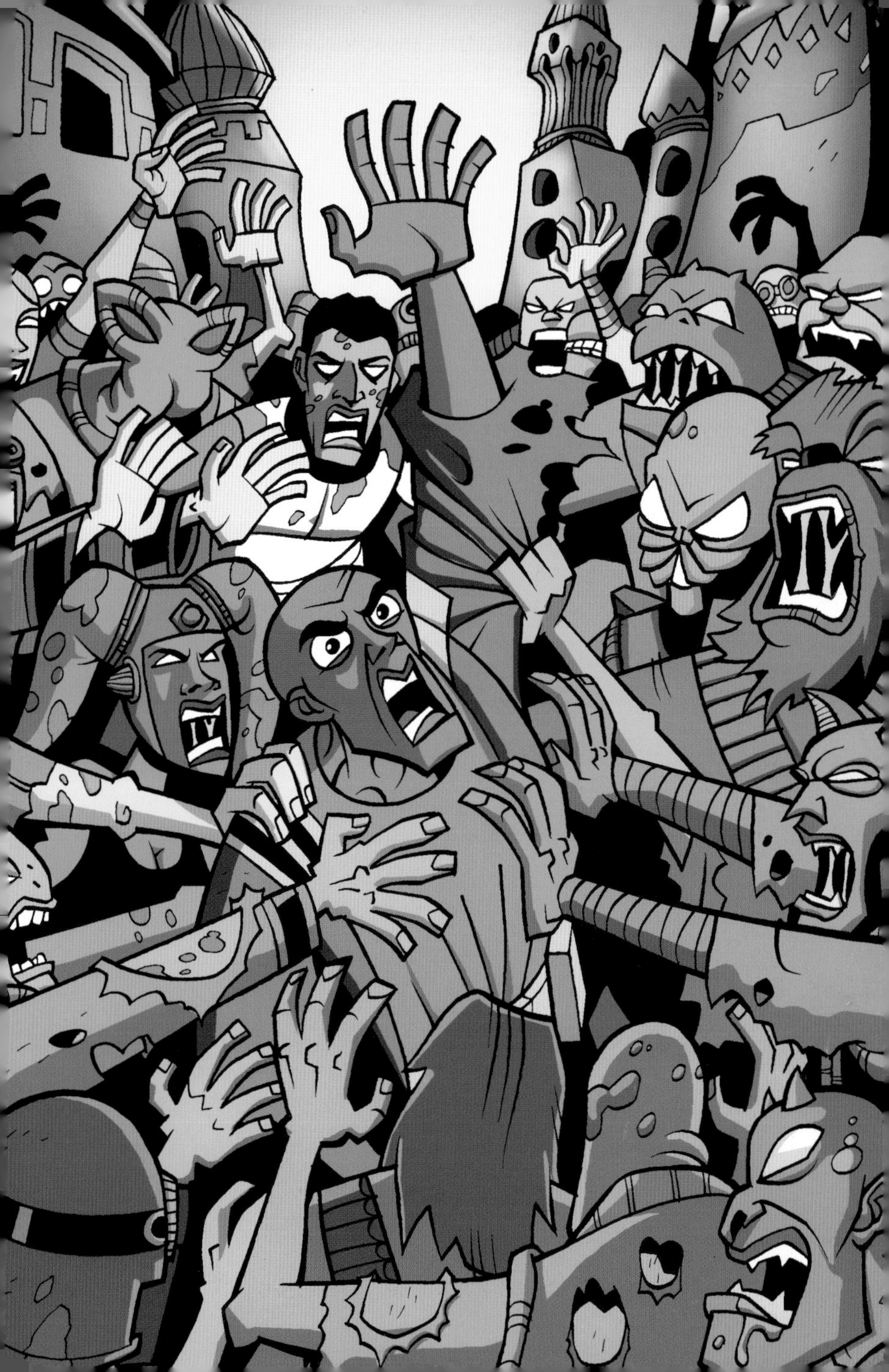

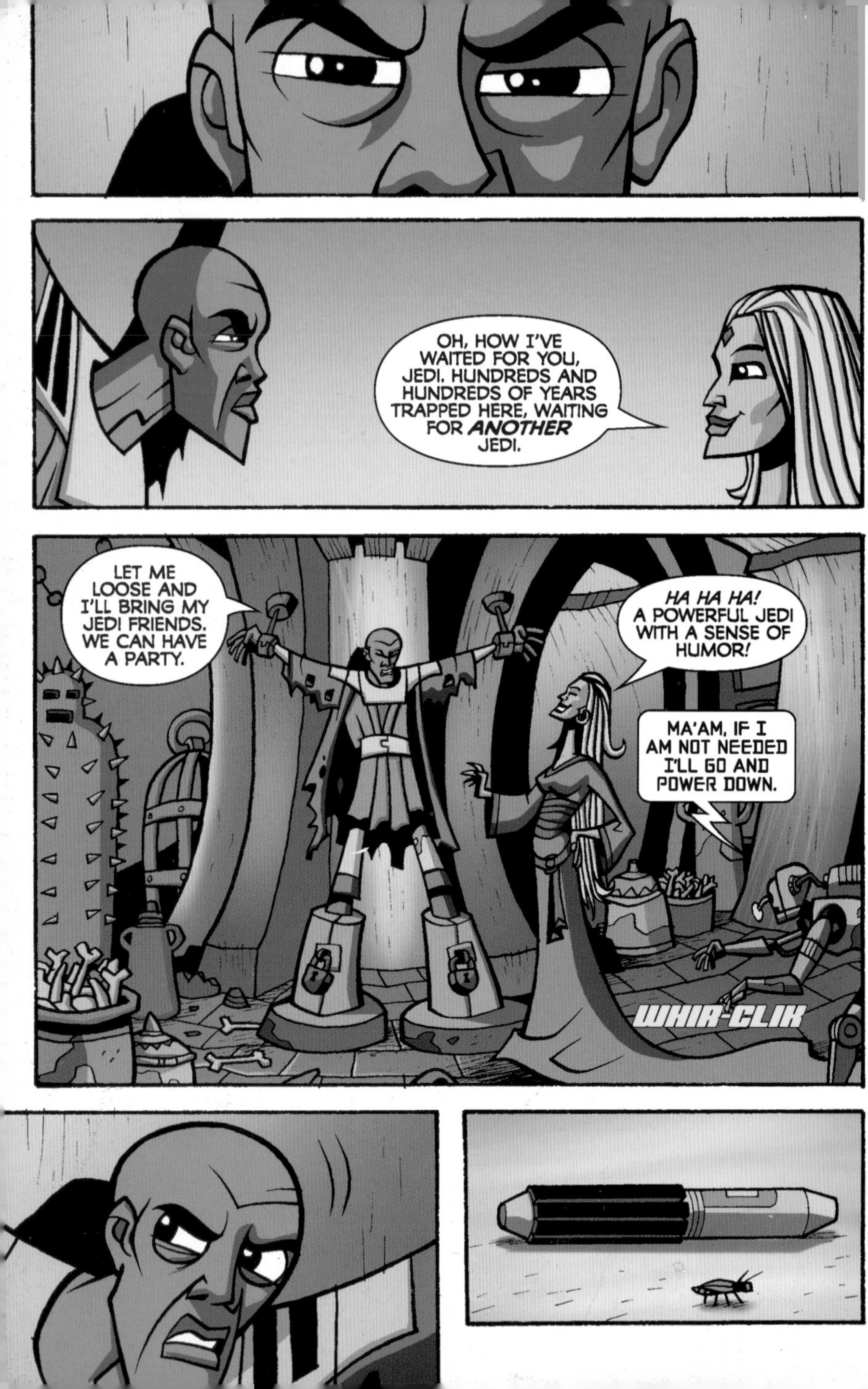
OH, HOW I'VE WAITED FOR YOU, JEDI. HUNDREDS AND HUNDREDS OF YEARS TRAPPED HERE, WAITING FOR ANOTHER JEDI.
LET ME LOOSE AND I'LL BRING MY JEDI FRIENDS. WE CAN HAVE A PARTY.
HA HA HA! A POWERFUL JEDI WITH A SENSE OF HUMOR!
MA'AM, IF I AM NOT NEEDED I'LL GO AND POWER DOWN.
WHIR-CLIK

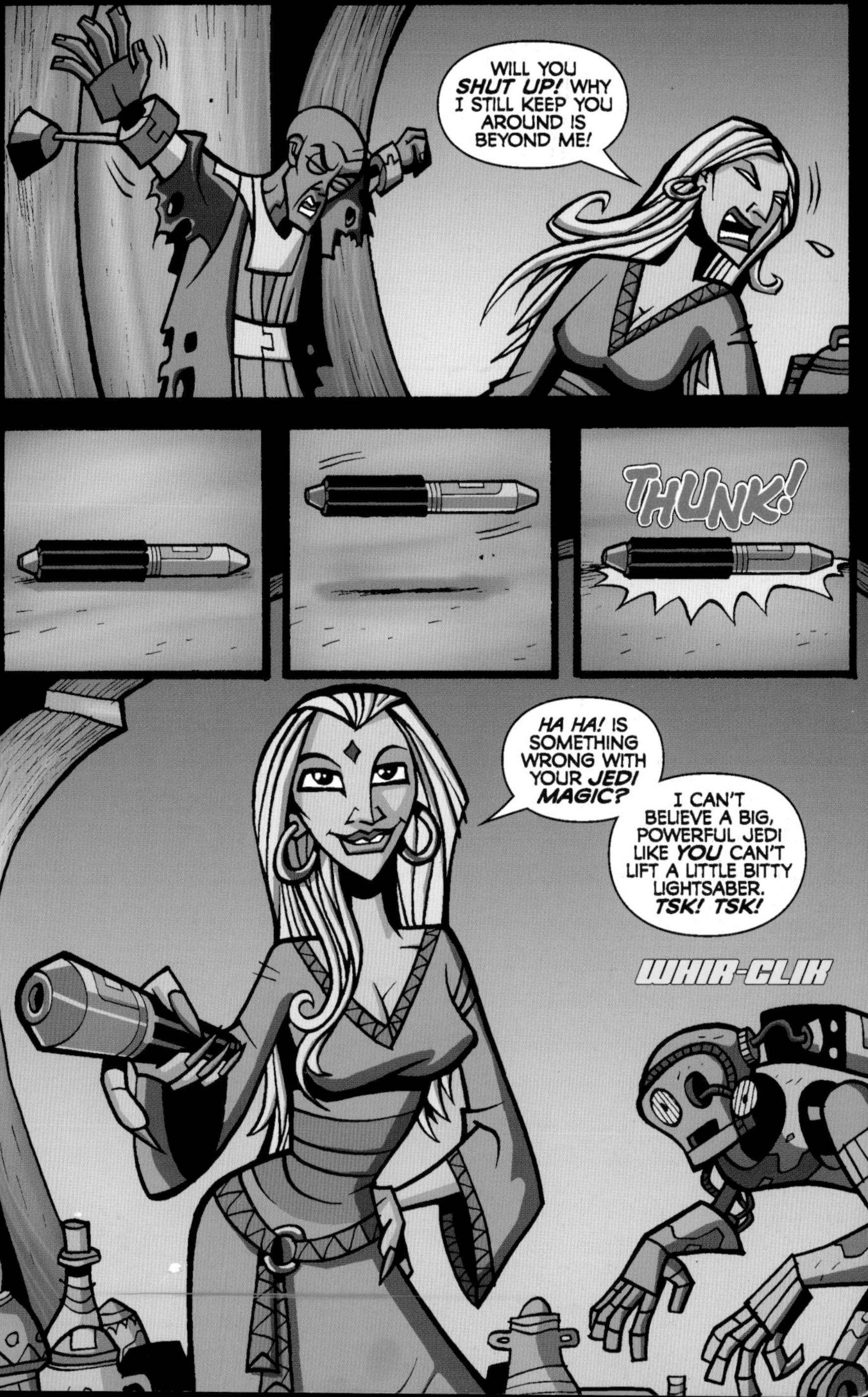
WILL YOU SHUT UP! WHY I STILL KEEP YOU AROUND IS BEYOND ME!
THUNK!
HA HA! IS SOMETHING WRONG WITH YOUR JEDI MAGIC?
I CAN'T BELIEVE A BIG, POWERFUL JEDI LIKE YOU CAN'T LIFT A LITTLE BITTY LIGHTSABER. TSK! TSK!
WHIR-CLIK

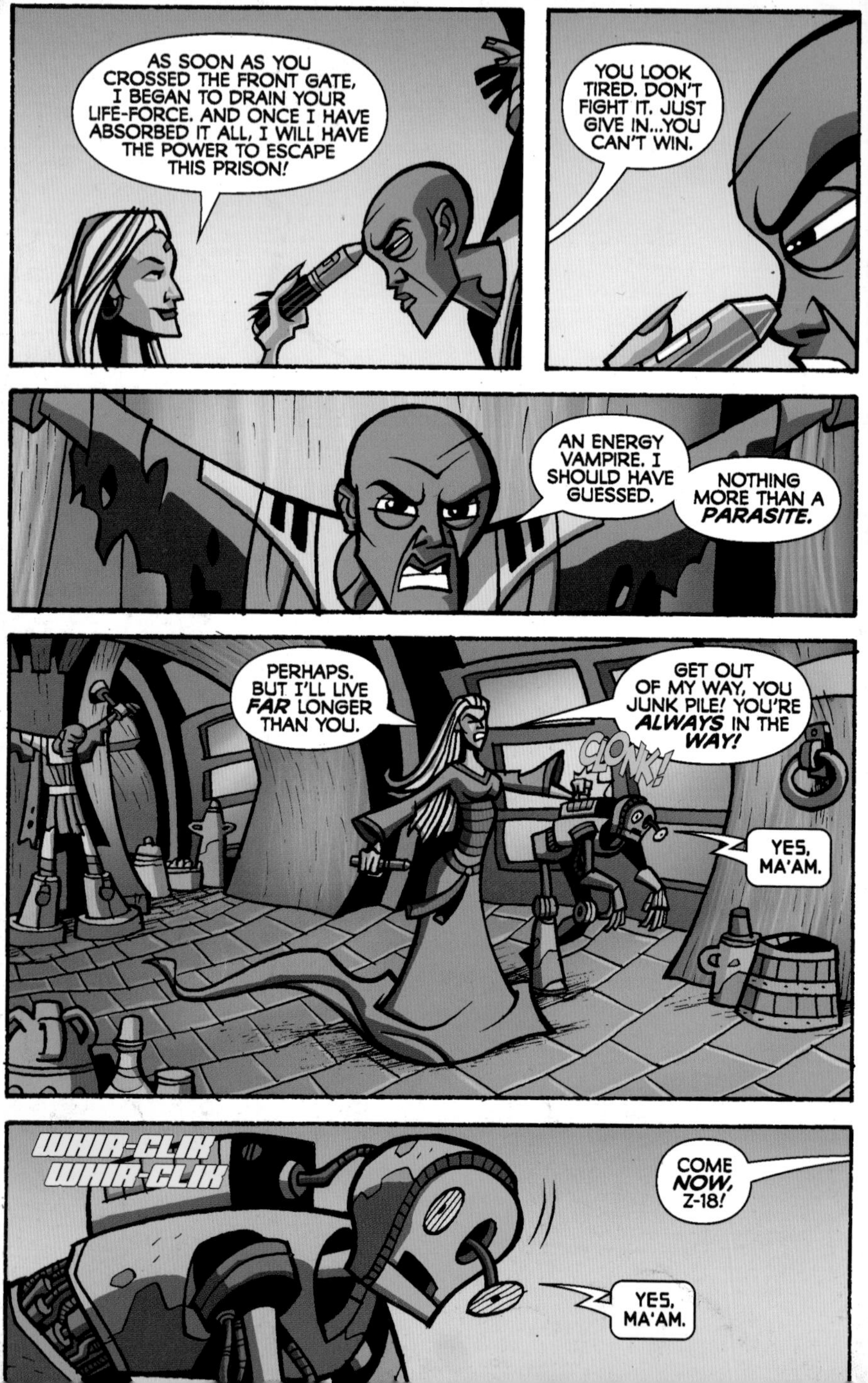
AS SOON AS YOU CROSSED THE FRONT GATE, I BEGAN TO DRAIN YOUR LIFE-FORCE. AND ONCE I HAVE ABSORBED IT ALL, I WILL HAVE THE POWER TO ESCAPE THIS PRISON!
YOU LOOK TIRED. DON'T FIGHT IT. JUST GIVE IN...YOU CAN'T WIN.
AN ENERGY VAMPIRE. I SHOULD HAVE GUESSED.
NOTHING MORE THAN A *PARASITE.*
PERHAPS. BUT I'LL LIVE *FAR* LONGER THAN YOU.
GET OUT OF MY WAY, YOU JUNK PILE! YOU'RE *ALWAYS* IN THE *WAY!*
CLONK!
YES, MA'AM.
WHIR-CLIK
WHIR-CLIK
COME *NOW,* Z-18!
YES, MA'AM.

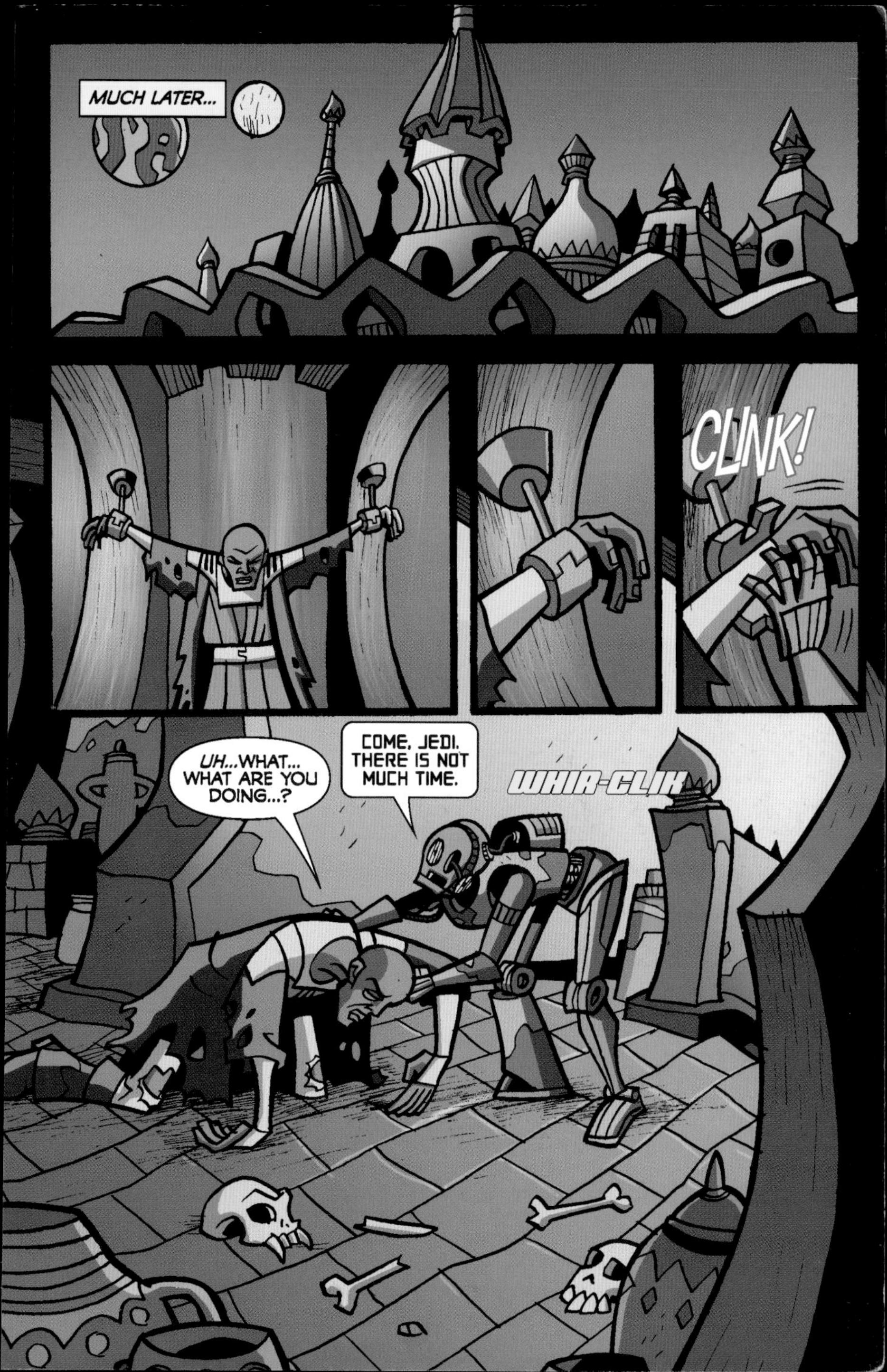
MUCH LATER...
CLINK!
UH...WHAT... WHAT ARE YOU DOING...?
COME, JEDI. THERE IS NOT MUCH TIME.
WHIR-CLIK

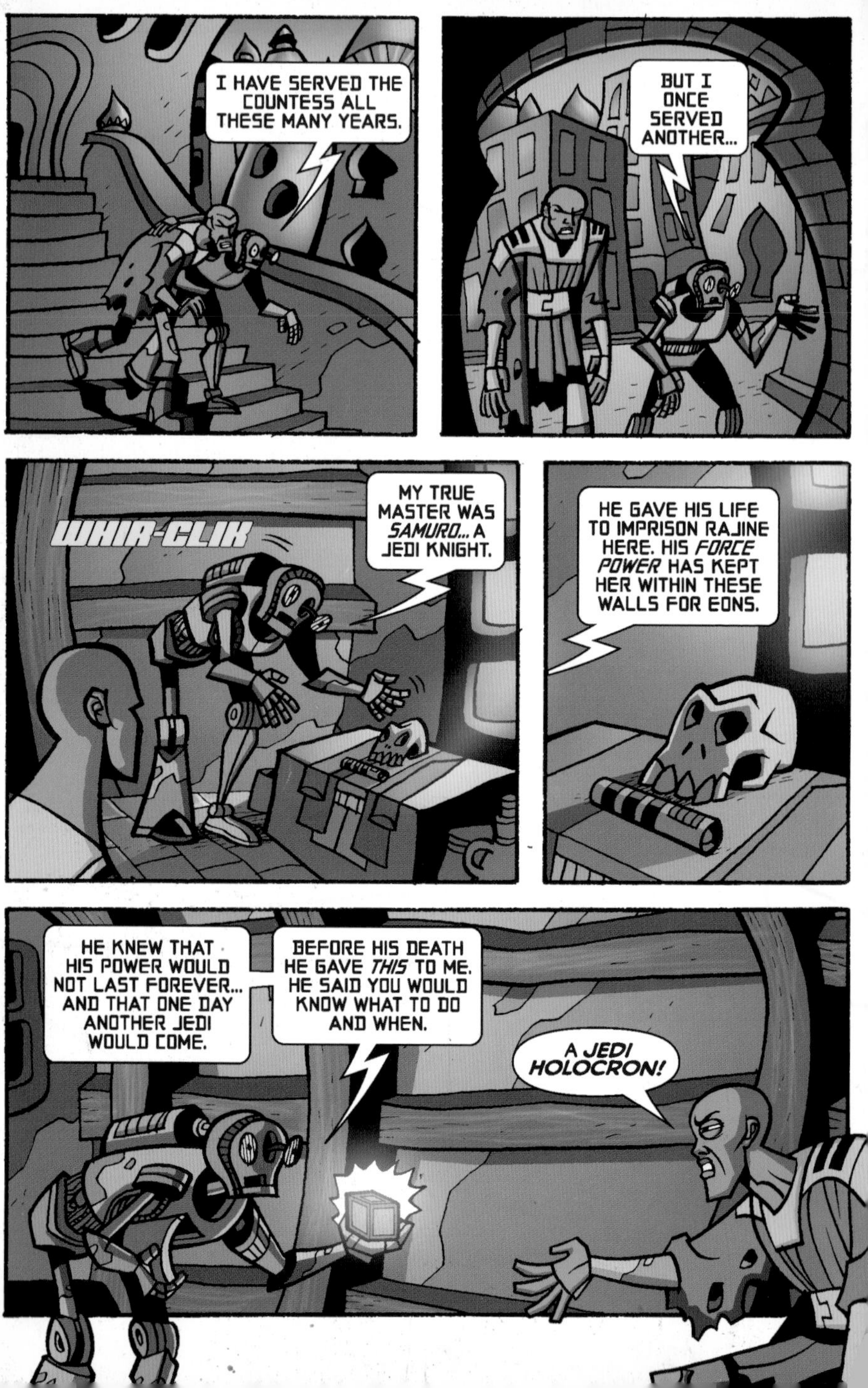
I HAVE SERVED THE COUNTESS ALL THESE MANY YEARS.
BUT I ONCE SERVED ANOTHER...
WHIR-CLIK
MY TRUE MASTER WAS *SAMURO*... A JEDI KNIGHT.
HE GAVE HIS LIFE TO IMPRISON RAJINE HERE. HIS *FORCE POWER* HAS KEPT HER WITHIN THESE WALLS FOR EONS.
HE KNEW THAT HIS POWER WOULD NOT LAST FOREVER... AND THAT ONE DAY ANOTHER JEDI WOULD COME.
BEFORE HIS DEATH HE GAVE *THIS* TO ME. HE SAID YOU WOULD KNOW WHAT TO DO AND WHEN.
A *JEDI HOLOCRON!*

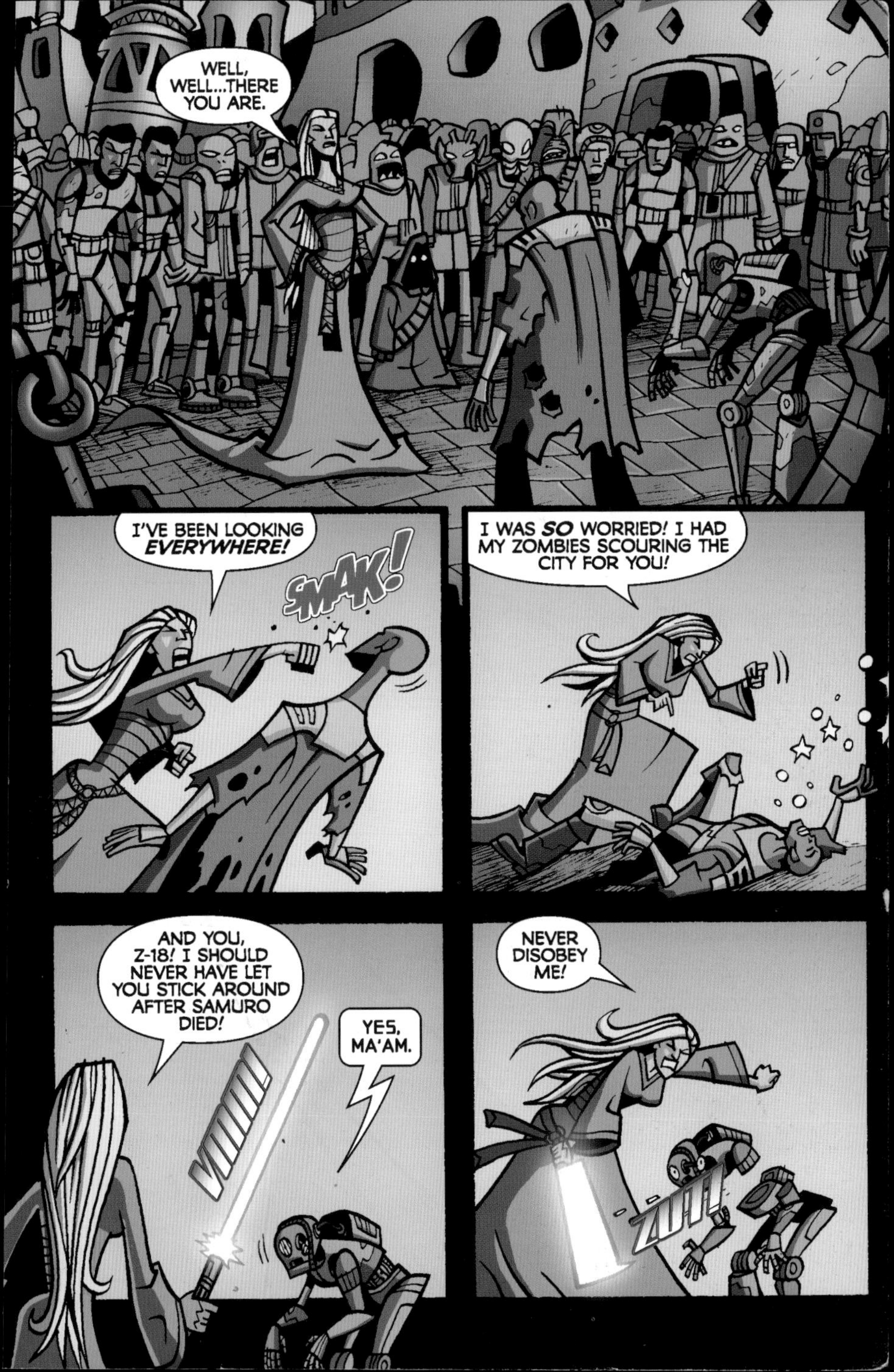
WELL, WELL...THERE YOU ARE.
I'VE BEEN LOOKING *EVERYWHERE!*
SMAK!
I WAS *SO* WORRIED! I HAD MY ZOMBIES SCOURING THE CITY FOR YOU!
AND YOU, Z-18! I SHOULD NEVER HAVE LET YOU STICK AROUND AFTER SAMURO DIED!
YES, MA'AM.
NEVER DISOBEY ME!
ZOT!

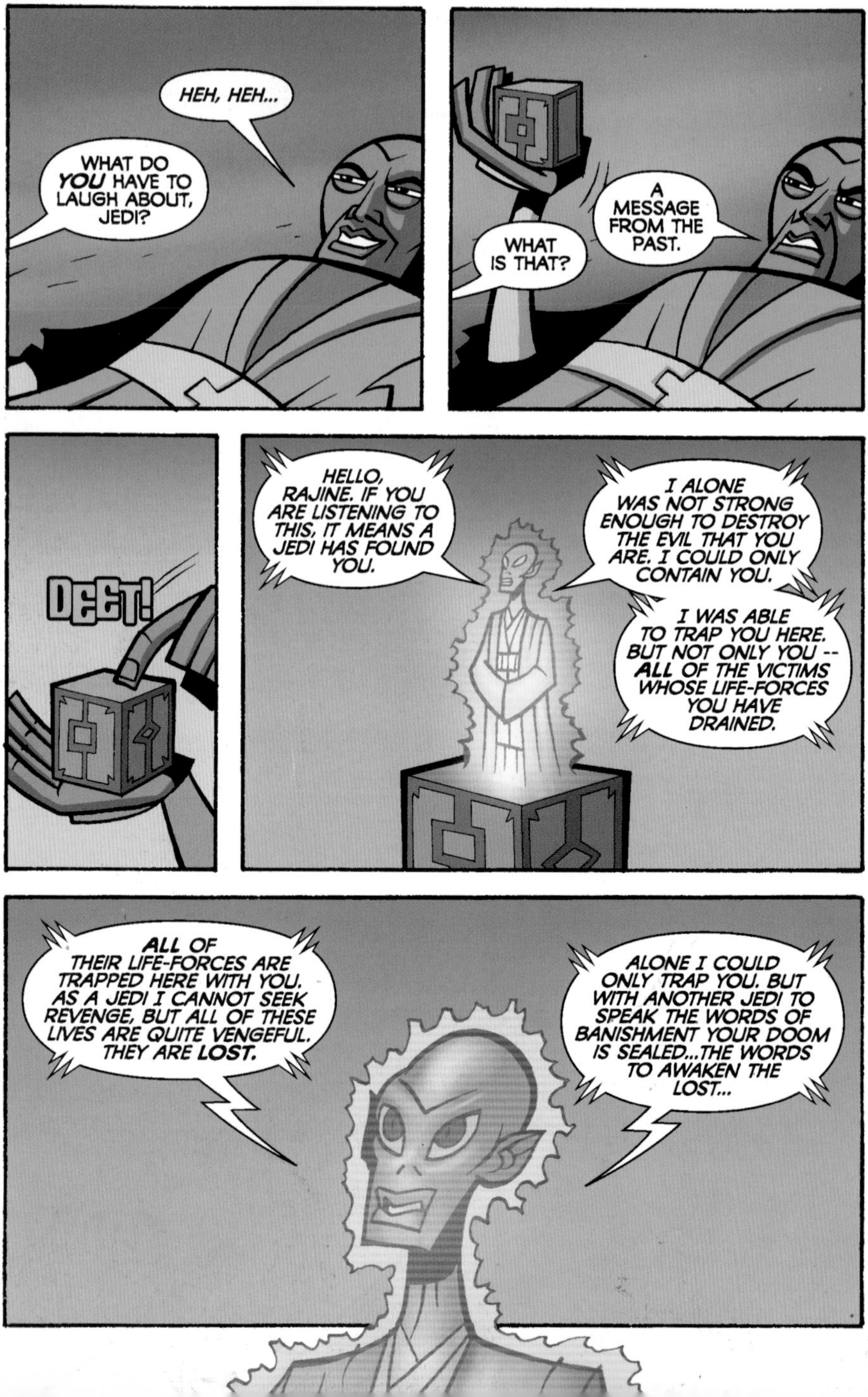
HEH, HEH...
WHAT DO YOU HAVE TO LAUGH ABOUT, JEDI?
WHAT IS THAT?
A MESSAGE FROM THE PAST.
DEET!
HELLO, RAJINE. IF YOU ARE LISTENING TO THIS, IT MEANS A JEDI HAS FOUND YOU.
I ALONE WAS NOT STRONG ENOUGH TO DESTROY THE EVIL THAT YOU ARE. I COULD ONLY CONTAIN YOU.
I WAS ABLE TO TRAP YOU HERE. BUT NOT ONLY YOU -- ALL OF THE VICTIMS WHOSE LIFE-FORCES YOU HAVE DRAINED.
ALL OF THEIR LIFE-FORCES ARE TRAPPED HERE WITH YOU. AS A JEDI I CANNOT SEEK REVENGE, BUT ALL OF THESE LIVES ARE QUITE VENGEFUL. THEY ARE LOST.
ALONE I COULD ONLY TRAP YOU. BUT WITH ANOTHER JEDI TO SPEAK THE WORDS OF BANISHMENT YOUR DOOM IS SEALED...THE WORDS TO AWAKEN THE LOST...

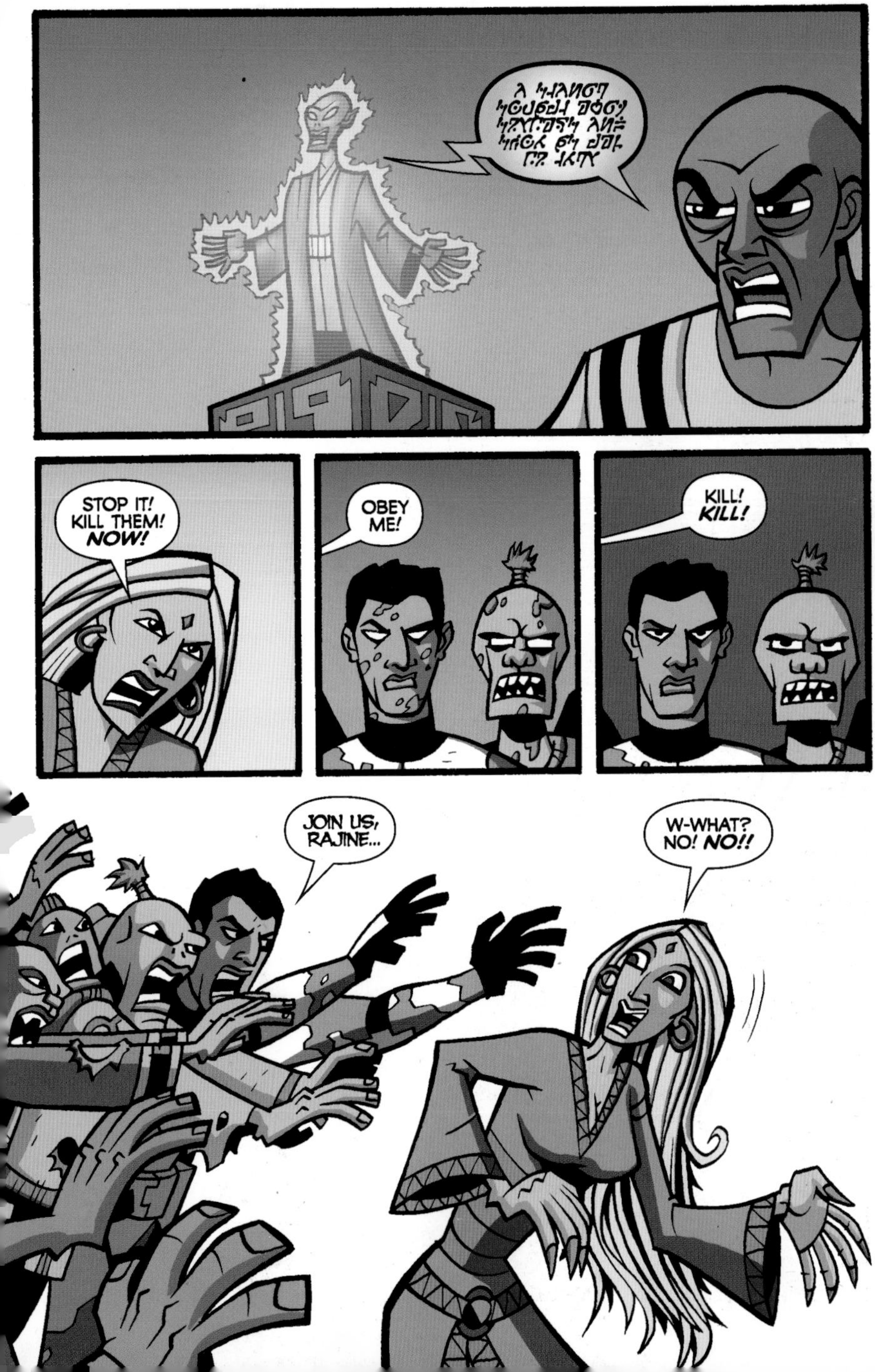
STOP IT! KILL THEM! NOW!
OBEY ME!
KILL! KILL!
JOIN US, RAJINE...
W-WHAT? NO! NO!!

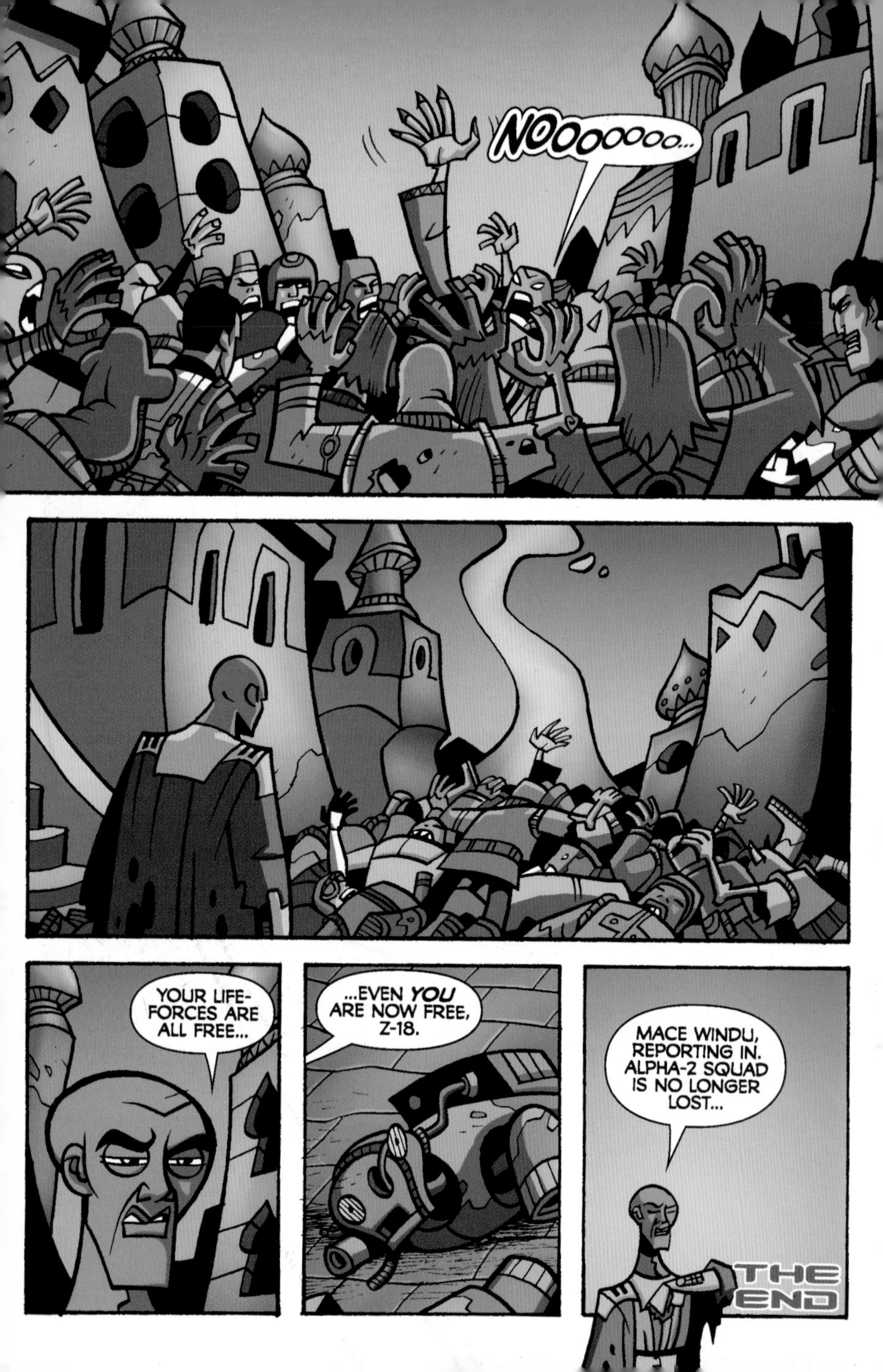
NOOOOOOO...
YOUR LIFE-FORCES ARE ALL FREE...
...EVEN *YOU* ARE NOW FREE, Z-18.
MACE WINDU, REPORTING IN. ALPHA-2 SQUAD IS NO LONGER LOST...
THE END

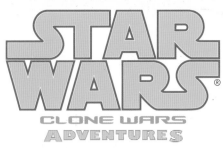

STAR WARS®
CLONE WARS ADVENTURES

Don't miss any of the action-packed adventures of your favorite STAR WARS® characters, available at comics shops and bookstores in a galaxy near you!

STAR WARS
CLONE WARS ADVENTURES
THREE NEW STORIES! ALL-JEDI ACTION!

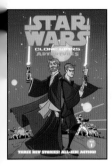

Volume 1
ISBN-10: 1-59307-243-0
ISBN-13: 978-1-59307-243-8

STAR WARS
CLONE WARS ADVENTURES
THREE TALES OF HYPERKINETIC JEDI ACTION!

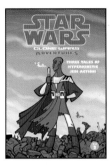

Volume 2
ISBN-10: 1-59307-271-6
ISBN-13: 978-1-59307-271-1

STAR WARS
CLONE WARS ADVENTURES
FOUR TALES OF SINISTER SEPARATIST SCHEMING AND ROCKING REPUBLIC COMBAT!

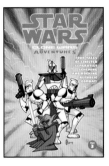

Volume 3
ISBN-10: 1-59307-307-0
ISBN-13: 978-1-59307-307-7

STAR WARS
CLONE WARS ADVENTURES
FOUR RIVETING ADVENTURES IN ONE FANTASTIC VOLUME!

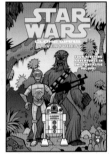

Volume 4
ISBN-10: 1-59307-402-6
ISBN-13: 978-1-59307-402-9

STAR WARS
CLONE WARS ADVENTURES
FOUR AMAZING TALES OF HEROISM AND GALAXY-SHAKING ACTION!

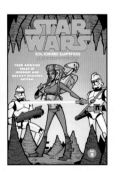

Volume 5
ISBN-10: 1-59307-483-2
ISBN-13: 978-1-59307-483-8

STAR WARS
CLONE WARS ADVENTURES
FOUR TALES OF PLANETS IN PERIL AND JEDI IN JEOPARDY!

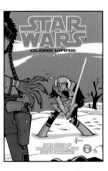

Volume 6
ISBN-10: 1-59307-567-7
ISBN-13: 978-1-59307-567-5

STAR WARS
CLONE WARS ADVENTURES

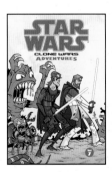

Volume 7
ISBN-10: 1-59307-678-9
ISBN-13: 978-1-59307-678-8

STAR WARS
CLONE WARS ADVENTURES

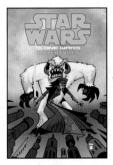

Volume 8
ISBN-10: 1-59307-680-0
ISBN-13: 978-1-59307-680-1
Coming in June!

$6.95 each!

To find a comics shop in your area, call 1-888-266-4226
For more information or to order direct: • On the web: darkhorse.com • Phone: 1-800-862-0052 Mon.-Fri. 9 A.M. to 5 P.M. Pacific Time.
• E-mail: mailorder@darkhorse.com *Prices and availability subject to change without notice.

STAR WARS®
CLONE WARS

Experience all the excitement and drama of the
Clone Wars! Look for these trade paperbacks at
a comics shop or book store near you!

VOLUME 1: THE DEFENSE OF KAMINO
ISBN-10: 1-56971-962-4
ISBN-13: 978-1-56971-962-6
$14.95

VOLUME 2: VICTORIES AND SACRIFICES
ISBN-10: 1-56971-969-1
ISBN-13: 978-1-56971-969-5
$14.95

VOLUME 3: LAST STAND ON JABIIM
ISBN-10: 1-59307-006-3
ISBN-13: 978-1-59307-006-9
$14.95

VOLUME 4: LIGHT AND DARK
ISBN-10: 1-59307-195-7
ISBN-13: 978-1-59307-195-0
$16.95

VOLUME 5: THE BEST BLADES
ISBN-10: 1-59307-273-2
ISBN-13: 978-1-59307-273-5
$14.95

VOLUME 6: ON THE FIELDS OF BATTLE
ISBN-10: 1-59307-352-6
ISBN-13: 978-1-59307-352-7
$17.95

VOLUME 7: WHEN THEY WERE BROTHERS
ISBN-10: 1-59307-396-8
ISBN-13: 978-1-59307-396-1
$17.95

VOLUME 8: THE LAST SIEGE, THE FINAL TRUTH
ISBN-10: 1-59307-482-4
ISBN-13: 978-1-59307-482-1
$17.95

VOLUME 9: ENDGAME
ISBN-10: 1-59307-553-7
ISBN-13: 978-1-59307-553-8
$17.95

To find a comics shop in your area, call 1-888-266-4226
For more information or to order direct:
• On the web: darkhorse.com
• E-mail: mailorder@darkhorse.com
• Phone: 1-800-862-0052
Mon.-Fri. 9 A.M. to 5 P.M. Pacific Time
*Prices and availability subject to change
without notice. STAR WARS © 2006
Lucasfilm Ltd. & ™ (BL8018)